MW00685125

KNOWLEDGE, TRUTH, AND SERVICE

The New York Botanical Garden, 1891 to 1980

Harry M. Dunkak

University Press of America,® Inc.
Lanham · Boulder · New York · Toronto · Plymouth, UK

Copyright © 2007 by
University Press of America,® Inc.
4501 Forbes Boulevard
Suite 200
Lanham, Maryland 20706
UPA Acquisitions Department (301) 459-3366

Estover Road
Plymouth PL6 7PY
United Kingdom

Library of Congress Control Number: 2007930028
ISBN-13: 978-0-7618-3839-5 (clothbound : alk. paper)
ISBN-10: 0-7618-3839-2 (clothbound : alk. paper)
ISBN-13: 978-0-7618-3840-1 (paperback : alk. paper)
ISBN-10: 0-7618-3840-6 (paperback : alk. paper)

Front cover photos: *top*, Haupt Conservatory; *bottom*, Native Forest

⊖™ The paper used in this publication meets the minimum
requirements of American National Standard for Information
Sciences—Permanence of Paper for Printed Library Materials,
ANSI Z39.48—1984

Table of Contents

Forward

An oasis in its urban environment, the New York Botanical Garden is considered to be among New York City's most venerated institutions. For well over a century, the New York Botanical Garden has remained faithful to its founding mission and New York State—granted charter, providing the city's inhabitants with a place to enjoy and learn about the diversity and beauty of the planet's plant life and provide the scientific community with cutting—edge research through its International Plant Science Center.

While this dimension of the Garden is well known to many, fewer may be aware of the Garden's role in preserving a piece of New York City's historical past. Occupying the site of the former estate of the Lorillard tobacco family, the Garden holds the designation of a National Historic Landmark.

Brother Harry Dunkak, Emeritus Professor of History at Iona College in New Rochelle, New York, has researched and masterfully captured that history and presents it to us in this historically accurate and well—documented monograph. This book is sure to find its way onto the shelves of all those interested in or connected to the New York Botanical Garden, in whatever capacity. Whether research scientist, history buff, Garden member, or occasional stroller through the Garden grounds, everyone is sure to be engaged and informed as Brother Dunkak takes us on an historical journey of this treasured piece of New York City real estate and the world renowned institution that sits upon it.

As he did in his earlier works on the history of the Irish laborers who helped build New York City's water supply system, the author captures an important element of our region's historical record in a style that is both informative and entertaining.

Warren Rosenberg, Ph.D.
Provost & Vice President for Academic Affairs
Professor of Biology
Iona College
New Rochelle, NY

Preface

While completing my doctoral degree at St. John's University, I was impressed by the knowledge, expertise and suggestions of Doctor James Bunce, Professor of History. This learned man stressed to me the importance of researching and publishing local history, especially the New York area. He believed that this locale afforded the historian a fascinating and bountiful area for research. With this suggestion and under his mentorship I completed my doctoral dissertation on John Morin Scott, an important mid—18th New Yorker who became a leader in the struggle against Great Britain.

Dr. Bunce's suggestions have led me to concentrate my own research and publications on local history, especially that of Westchester County, New York. While researching the Lorillard Family I visited the library of the New York Botanical Garden. The Lorillards owned the property that eventually became The Garden. When I was informed of a need for a history of The Garden, I began my research on a study of that great institution. My thanks to The Garden's librarians for their indispensable assistance and to Dr. Brian Boom, Vice President for Scientific Research, for his encouragement and support.

The editor of *The Westchester Historian* has kindly granted permission for me to use the Lorillard article in this present monograph. The contents of this article entitled: "The Lorillard Family of Westchester County: Tobacco, Property and Nature" appear with a few changes in Chapter II of The Garden history.

Acknowledgements

This study of the New York Botanical Garden would never have been published without the encouragement and support of Iona College in New Rochelle, New York. In particular my sincere appreciation goes to Doctor Warren Rosenberg, Provost, Vice President of Academic Affairs at Iona College and Doctor Alex Eodice, Iona's Dean of Arts and Science for their assistance. I especially thank Doctor Rosenberg for writing the forward to this monograph.

My sincere gratitude is extended to Ms. Diana Breen, Iona College's Director of CELTIC (The Center for Enhancement of Learning and Teaching at Iona College). Diana Breen, with her extensive knowledge and expertise, graciously and cheerfully spent many hours with me in the preparation of this history of The New York Botanical garden and instructing me in the intricacies of Microsoft Word. My appreciation is also extended to Elpida Halaris, Osarieme Uwaifo and Eric Jackson, staff members of CELTIC for their assistance in the preparation and completion of the Index to this study.

I am especially indebted to the Reverend Brother Charles B. Quinn, Emeritus Professor of English at Iona College, former Dean of the School of Arts and Science, former Executive Vice President for Academic Affairs and Past Grand Marshall of the famous New York City St. Patrick's Day Parade, for proofreading the manuscript and offering invaluable suggestions for the final text.

Introduction

The New York Botanical Garden was established by an enactment of the New York State Legislature signed by the Governor on April 28, 1891. This 1891 Act of Incorporation, amended by the Legislature on March 7, 1894, marked the beginning of the official history of The Garden. For a copy of the 1894 amended Act of Incorporation, see Appendix A.

The Act of Incorporation set forth the purposes and objectives for which The New York Botanical Garden was established. As stated in the Act of Incorporation there were four objectives which the institution was obligated to maintain and fully develop during the course of its growth.

1) Establish and maintain a botanical garden, museum and arboretum for the collection and cultivation of plants, flowers, shrubs and trees.

2) Advance the field of botany and scientific knowledge through original research, which would include the organization and leadership of expeditions for the better awareness and understanding of the earth's plant life,

3) Offer courses of instruction in horticulture, gardening and plant life.

4) Provide a place of entertainment, where the public may recreate and learn, formally and informally, about the beauties of plant life.

This historical study of The New York Botanical Garden was written to provide a comprehensive history of this great, vital institution. The monograph is intended for the general public as well as the scientific community; that is, all who are interested in the story of this fascinating and vitally important public, service organization. In order to familiarize the reader with the nature and historical development of the modern botanical garden, the narration begins long before 1891. In addition, this account relates the interesting history of the locality and the people who inhabited the area where this great botanical institution was established. The chronicle of The Garden also includes a description of the fascinating origin of the notion of a botanical garden for New York, a picture of this rapidly evolving metropolis of the late nineteenth century and the establishment and early development of this institution in this great City, despite many obstacles. The conclusion of this history of the New York Botanical Garden takes the reader down to the major events of the late 1970s, with an overview of the Garden in 2000.

Botanical gardens have always played a significant role in the story of the human race. They have provided mankind with the knowledge that has increased and enhanced the length and quality of human life, as well as a sanctuary from the everyday cares of normal human existence. As the earth's population has become more urbanized, botanical gardens have taken on an even greater importance. Increasingly they have become recognized not only as scientific and academic enclaves, but have become cultural resources similar in value to museums devoted to the arts and to concert halls for musical presentations. As cities have become metropolises, and in the very near future megalopolises if this phenomenon has not already occurred in some areas of the world, botanical gardens offer to the urban inhabitant views of the natural world which are no longer accessible. They offer a mental, emotional and aesthetic escape from the pressures inherent in urban life, a type of existence that tends to overwhelm its inhabitants. Botanical Gardens can also suggest to the visitors new interests and hobbies that never before entered their minds. Providing new outlets, even if they only mean the study and reading about plant life, can open whole new worlds for the urban inhabitant. Every institution or organization has a mission, even if in the case of a corporation the objective is merely to make money. The mission of a botanical garden is to provide public service. It is an institution that is missioned to seek, develop and provide information and a locale to improve human existence. In the case of The New York Botanical Garden this mission or objective has almost taken on a sacred connotation. The Garden not only has a mission but there is a certain charisma that permeates its very foundation, development and history. This charisma is not easily seen or defined, but it is nevertheless present. Reading the history of The New York Botanical Garden makes present this special charisma that has characterized this great institution down through the years since its inception back in the nineteenth century.

Chapter I: History of Gardens

A botanical garden is more than a place to admire beautiful plants, stately trees and well—situated gardens. In the ancient Egypt of more than five thousand years ago there were beautiful gardens, but they cannot be considered botanic gardens since they were developed only for aesthetic reasons. Thus the famous gardens of ancient Karnak, Egypt, however beautiful they may have been, cannot be called botanical gardens. History records that wealthy Romans developed spacious and beautiful gardens at their country villas, but they were not designed for scientific objectives. These Romans were not botanists; their gardens were not used for analysis, but for the gathering of valuable plants for viewing purposes. Although the aesthetic significance of a botanical garden cannot be dismissed, they are designed primarily for research, study and the dissemination of knowledge.[1]

There is some debate over the development of the first botanical garden, but it is generally presumed that Aristotle (384 to 322 B.C.) cultivated the first such garden. To Aristotle's school at the Lyceum in ancient Athens, Alexander the Great (356 to 323 B.C.) sent information about the flora sighted during his many conquests of the known world at that time. Aristotle was not only a philosopher, but also a natural scientist who had field workers sending information and plants for observation and study. Aristotle's famous pupil, Theophrastus (? to 287? B.C.) developed, close to the Lyceum, a museum that was actually a garden where botanical studies were conducted. His last will and testament gave his students and staff the necessary information for the care of the garden. Aristotle imbued Theophrastus (considered to be the father of botany) and his other students with an inquisitive mind about plant life, thus giving Aristotle first place in the development of botanical gardens.[2]

The ancient Chinese were also among the early founders of botanic gardens. History records that the Emperor Wu—Ti (140 to 86 B.C.) of the Han Dynasty brought northward tropical fruits such as the orange and the banana. By careful cultivation he was able to acclimate these trees to a different environment. Thus giving a scientific aspect to the garden.

When Hernan Cortez (1485—1547) conquered the Aztec Empire in

1519—1521, he came into contact with the well—established royal gardens of the Emperor Montezuma. Cortez reported that the gardens were systematically arranged and that the plants were used for medicinal purposes. By 1570 King Philip II of Spain had heard fabulous stories about the medicinal properties of the plant life of the Americas. In response to his curiosity the Spanish monarch sent his personal physician and botanist, Francisco Hernandez, to investigate. Hernandez' published work on the plants of the New World received wide notoriety and great acclaim among Europeans.[3]

In Europe during the Early Middle Ages the Christian monasteries were the centers of learning where works of theology, philosophy and literature were painstakingly preserved by the scribes. The monks were also vitally concerned with the care of the sick and thus cultivated medicinal gardens. Started in 820 AD. the physic gardens developed at the Benedictine Monastery of St. Gall in Switzerland were typical of those established by most of the monks and nuns of this period. Near the house of the so—called physician small rectangular herbal beds were established and carefully labeled. The garden products, mainly opium, poppy, squill, colocynth, savin and rue, were all considered to manifest medicinal qualities of a simple remedy. "This is the origin of the word 'simple' for a medicinal plant. From these vegetables, 'simplicia' or 'simple', the 'remedia composita' were prepared by the apothecaries." As a result the "physician" was also a horticulturist.[4]

In manuscript form the monastic scribes also kept records of the medicinal significance of the products of the herbal gardens. With the invention of the printing press these works were widely disseminated, especially those books of the monasteries at Brunfels, Bock and Fuchs. The books were called herbals and became the initial botany textbooks; and these medicinal gardens of the Middle Ages, cultivated within a small area on the monastery grounds, are considered to be the predecessors of the modern botanical gardens. These gardens were designed and operated for their utilitarian or economic value.

The first medicinal gardens on a grander scale were those founded under Pope Niccolo III (1277—1280). This pontiff established the Vatican as the fixed residence of the popes and created the Vatican Gardens, then called "Viridarium novum". A section of this magnificent garden was set aside for cultivating medicinal plants. Simone of Genoa, the personal physician to Pope Niccolo IV (1288—1292), had great confidence in and made great use of these medicinal plants. This is evident in his medical treatise, "Clavis sanitationis", where he writes of his experiences in transplanting various herbs. Pope Niccolo V (1447—1455) completed the creation of the Vatican Gardens. This great humanistic pontiff expanded the Gardens and began the Vatican Library that included medicinal treatises. The medical professors at the University of Rome, called "The Sapienza", made use of both the Vatican Gardens and the Vatican Library books in their lectures and demonstrations. This Vatican concept of a medicinal garden spread: Hamburg, Germany, in 1316; Salerno, Italy, in 1340;

Erfurt, Germany in 1525 and other parts of Europe where medical schools were located.[6]

These herbal gardens were not in the strict sense the modern botanical garden. They were not really scientific academies where research was conducted. In 1533, however, Francesco Bonafide established the first Chair of Simplis at the University of Padua (at that time Padua belonged to the Republic of Venice), therefore instituting the study of botany as a separate branch of instruction. In 1542 Bonafide petitioned the Venetian Senate to establish at Padua a botanical garden as an adjunct to the Department of Botany at the University. The Senate in 1545 granted the request and thus was established in Padua the first modern botanical garden, a place of observation and research. Almost concurrently a botanical garden was established in Pisa.[7] Under the patronage of the Grand Duke Cosimo I di Medici of Florence, Luca Ghini created a botanical garden at Pisa. In turn, Andrea Cesalpino (1519—1603), a pupil of Ghini, devoted much of his life to the study of botany and was the long—time director of the botanic garden at Bologna (established 1568). In 1583 Cesalpino published *De Plantis* that set forth the initial system of plant classification. This publication, although based more on speculation than observation (Cesalpino was trained as a philosopher) and of dubious scientific importance, did, however, help to stimulate interest in the new science of botany. By 1800 the following botanical gardens of considerable importance (there were others) were founded in Europe: Paris, 1591; Montpellier, 1598; Heidelberg, 1593; Geissen, 1605; Strassburg, 1620; Oxford, 1621; Jena, 1699; Upsala, 1657; Chelsea, 1673; Berlin, 1679; Edinburgh, 1680; Amsterdam, 1682; St. Petersburg, 1713; Vienna, 1754; Cambridge (England), 1762; Dublin (Ireland), 1790.

By the beginning of the eighteenth century, modern botany began to take shape.[8] Carolus Linnaeus, born Karl von Linne', (1707—1778) of Sweden, through his untiring work in a botanical garden, was able to develop a system of plant classification that became the norm for botanists. George Clifford (1685—1760), by profession the Director of the Dutch East India Company, became interested in botany as a hobby. At Hartecamp near Haarlem, The Netherlands, he established a botanical garden with a museum, library and herbarium and in 1735 hired Linne' as the curator. In a sense Linne' got his start with Clifford at Hartecamp and then in 1742 was appointed the Director of the Botanical Gardens at Upsala, Sweden, where he worked until his death in 1778. There were many other individuals and gardens, but it is a fact that the European Renaissance stimulated almost all fields of human endeavor, including that of the foundation and spread of research conducted in botanical gardens.[9]

Any description of the development of botanical gardens should include the Royal Botanic Gardens at Kew, a village suburb of London in Surrey, England. In 1730 Frederick, Prince of Wales, leased Kew House and began the development of the grounds that eventually became noted for their aesthetic attractions. Kew, however, remained merely an attraction as a pleasure garden and the repository of exotic plants until William Jackson Hooker was appointed the director in 1841. Coming from Glasgow, Scotland, he deposited his personal herbarium at Kew (by the 1950s the institution's herbarium collection had reached the astounding number of approximately five million specimens). Hooker and his staff collected and studied the flora to be found in all parts of the ever—expanding British Empire. Kew also engaged in the introduction of new plants for commercial use in the British Empire. Captain Bligh's famous voyage to the South Seas to collect the breadfruit for use as a food in the West Indies was sponsored by the Garden. In 1860 Kew organized the expedition to South America that introduced the quinine plant to India. From Brazil in 1875 Kew suggested the collection of seeds from the rubber tree. These seeds became the basis of the great rubber plantations of the British possessions in the Far East. Millions of people visit the Royal Botanic Gardens at Kew, but it has also been in the forefront of botanical exploration and research.[10]

In America the earliest gardens were not botanical but were physic gardens or were private gardens established by individuals interested in horticulture. Adriaen van der Donck's *Description of the New Netherlands* states that in New Amsterdam in 1653 a physic garden belonged to a surgeon, who obviously copied from those located in Holland. The Ursuline Order of Nuns arrived in New Orleans, Louisiana, early in the eighteenth century and by 1734 had built a convent with a medicinal garden.[11] Even the famous garden established in Philadelphia, Pennsylvania, by the celebrated John Bartram was not strictly speaking botanic in nature. In his travels throughout North America this well—known botanist collected plants, brought them back to Philadelphia and planted them. In 1760 he even built a greenhouse for his garden. Bartram, however, used no systematic planting method nor did he conduct research or teach botany. Although visited by many interested in plants, Bartram's enterprise was not a botanic garden and eventually became a nursery.[12]

In New York the Dutch who established New Amsterdam in 1624 carried with them from the Netherlands a keen interest and an adequate understanding of horticulture, especially as that pertains to farming. This does not mean that they were botanists or that early in their history in New Amsterdam they had established botanical gardens, but rather that a tradition of horticulture in New York had been established by the Dutch settlers.

In lower Manhattan the Bowery stretches for about one mile from Chatham Square to Cooper Square. The name is derived from the Dutch word, bowerij, which means farm. In the seventeenth century the bowery was an area of farms that supplied food for the Dutch settlement located in lower Manhattan. In 1651 Governor Peter Stuyvesant bought land in the bowery and established a farm. On this property, which he called the bouwerie, he planted many fruit trees from which grafts were taken for orchards along the Hudson River. On Staten Island the Dutch planted many orchards that were attacked by Native Americans in 1655 in a struggle known as the Peach War. A description of New Amsterdam includes the fact that behind the homes of the wealthy merchants there stretched fruit orchards and tulip gardens. Starting with the arrival of British in 1664 the Dutch congregated along the Hudson and Mohawk Rivers where they established large and successful agricultural estates; the area maintained its Dutch character of sober industriousness, with cultivated estates and farms, well into the twentieth century.[13]

The first commercial nursery in the American Colonies was established in Flushing, New York, in 1737 and specialized in raising fruit trees and ornamental scrubs. The noteworthy American portrait artist, John Singleton Copely (1738—1815), purchased from this nursery several types of plants, including mountain laurel, for his estate on Beacon Hill in Boston, Massachusetts. During the 1750s in what is now Queens, New York, the Newtown Pippin apple was developed, especially for a London, England, clientele. The first greenhouse in New York was constructed in 1764 by James Beekman (the scion of a famous American family) near the present 51st Street and 1st Avenue.[14]

A few years before the American Revolution the Linnean Botanic Garden was established in Flushing by William Prince and remained in the family for more than one hundred years. The Princes specialized in developing new strains of fruits, especially those of the plum variety. To their credit they developed the Imperial Gage, Red Gage, Prince's Gage and the Washington plum. By 1828 Prince's Nursery was offering one hundred and forty types of plums and could claim to have given the greatest impetus to the development and growth of plums in America.[15] The greatest impetus to horticultural development in New York City occurred in the late 1850s with the construction of Central Park. The Park introduced many new examples of flora to the City, including Japanese maples gathered by the American Commodore Matthew C. Perry (1794—1858) in his famous 1854 Japanese expedition that opened that Far Eastern nation to the Western World.[16]

The first important work in the study of botany in New York was conducted in the eighteenth century by the celebrated scholar and humanist, Cadwallader Colden (1688—1776). Trained as a doctor in Edinburgh and London, he practiced medicine in Philadelphia before coming to New York in 1718. Colden became very active in politics, rising to the rank of Lieutenant Governor of New York. He also achieved notoriety in anthropology through his studies of the Iroquois and the subsequent publication of *The History of the Five Indian Nations Depending on the Province of New York* (1727), a study still considered of vital importance in understanding those Native Americans. In the study of botany he was aided by his daughter Jane (1724—1766), a celebrated botanist in her own right. On the family estate near Newburgh, New York, father and daughter developed botanical gardens and carried—on their studies. Through correspondence he came to know Charles Linnaeus, Benjamin Franklin, Samuel Johnson and others avidly interested in any form of study. His correspondence with other botanists resulted not only in an exchange of knowledge, but also the acquisition of foreign specimens that were cultivated on his Newburgh estate. Upon learning the Linnean system, Colden published in 1749 a scientific study on the classification of New York plant life[17]

In 1801 there occurred an event of the greatest importance in the development of botanical gardens and the science of botany in New York ——the opening of the Elgin Botanical Garden. Established by David Hosack, a physician and second professor of botany at Columbia University, the Elgin Garden was the first public botanical garden in the United States. With his own funds he acquired twenty acres of land in an area now bounded by 46th and 50th Streets and 5th and Madison Avenues.

David Hosack's noteworthy contribution was his approach to botany and the use of botanical gardens. Like most physicians of his time, Hosack's interest in botany was mainly medical. The chemical make—up of plants at that time, of course, was almost entirely unknown. In addition, the medicinal value of plants was obtained by the reaction and report of the patient and the practioner. This process is certainly empirical in nature, but obviously not very reliable or necessarily accurate. Hosack's great contribution was that he realized that something more was needed. And that something was the conviction that the accurate knowledge of plant life and a sound botany course required an observation of growing plants. To conduct this research Hosack hired the most renowned botanist and taxonomist of that era, Frederick Pursh, to act as gardener and researcher on his newly purchased property. Pursh achieved his fame helping to identify plants gathered in the northwestern part of the United States by the famous Lewis and Clark Expedition in 1803 to 1806. Hosack erected a conservatory on the grounds of his garden and the Linnean and Jussieu systems were both used in the arrangement of his plants. As a research facility the Elgin Gardens are considered by many to be the predecessor to the New York Botanical Garden.

Hosack operated the Garden on very limited funds, but was very successful in the operation. By 1805 he had 1,500 valuable plants, some of them of the rare and exotic variety. There was a herbarium and nursery containing plants from all climes, gracefully arranged and meticulously labeled. The Garden had become successful in its research and popularity with the public, but the burden of maintenance was too much for the founder. By 1810 the garden had become a financial burden and Hosack persuaded the State of New York to purchase the property. In turn the State leased the Garden to the Columbia College of Physicians and Surgeons. Interest in the operation, however, declined as property values in the area increased. Elgin Gardens was eventually abandoned and the property became part of the fabulously valuable Rockefeller Center.[18]

The historical development of botanical gardens demonstrates that the function and purpose of these gardens have changed over the centuries. Nathaniel Lord Britton, the founder and first director of the New York Botanical Garden, pointed out that this development has led to the modern botanical garden as having four main elements:

1. The aesthetic
2. The utilitarian or economic
3. The scientific or biologic
4. The philanthropic[19]

The modern garden must be appealing to the public with the plants, shrubs and trees exhibited in a beautiful park—like setting. It should contain plants that grow well in that particular area. In this regard the botanical garden should be able to provide horticultural information for local gardeners and nurseries. "It would also be ideal to have a plant clinic to which persons could bring diseased plants for expert advice and information." The garden should also serve as a classroom by offering courses and programs for the amateur gardeners, the more advanced students and the experts interested in graduate studies. Furthermore, it is advisable for the garden to be associated with local institutions of higher learning. The Missouri Botanical Garden has had a close relationship with George Washington University and The New York Botanical Garden with Columbia and other universities. Most importantly the botanical garden should be a center for research. This would include the development of new varieties of plants, especially those of great importance to the human family. The collection and study of plants and herbaria should be used to increase our comprehension of the role plants play in the life of the human race. This function is carried out in the field and in the laboratory. All of these elements require funding; hence the philanthropic need for public and private funding for botanical gardens.[20]

Chapter II: History of the Bronx River Area

Of the geological formations within The New York Botanical Garden there are three basic types of rock:

Manhattan schist

Inwood limestone or dolomite

Fordham gneiss

These rock specimens were originally accumulated as sediment when the Bronx River Valley was covered by an ocean about 600 million years ago. Then the rock formations were hardened by pressure and metamorphosed by the action of heat and moisture. The Manhattan schist predominates, with only traces of Fordham gneiss on the western edges of the Garden near the Harlem Division of the New York Central Railroad. The Inwood limestone does not appear on the surface of any place within the Garden. At one time there was an outcrop of limestone near the main conservatory, but this was covered over during the process of grading that area. The distinctive and attractive hills and precipices within the Garden's confines were formed by pressures from beneath the surface of the earth.[1]

Flowing through The New York Botanical Garden is the Bronx River, hardly a river for it is navigable only by canoe or some such small vessel for most of its length. Larger vessels can navigate only the last 2.6 miles of the waterway, before it empties into the East River. Beginning on a hill in the Town of New Castle some six hundred and fifty feet above sea level the Bronx River flows some thirty miles southward through Westchester County and the Bronx which is part of New York City.[2] The Bronx River began to evolve some ten to twelve thousand years ago with the melting of the last glacier to cover this area. At first the Bronx River emptied into the Harlem River, but a huge piece of ice diverted the passage of the River through the Botanical Garden to empty into the East River between Clason's Point on the North and Hunt's Point on the South.

The Bronx River drains an area of some 56.4 miles, with tributaries of over 80 miles. The final 12 miles of the River are the most beautiful and dramatic. Part of this journey is through the Botanical Garden where the River flows through a narrow, magnificent gorge that is one hundred feet high with a scenic waterfall at the bottom of the gorge. The scene is reminiscent of one pictured in the Catskill Mountains in Central New York State and not in the City of New York.

With a temperate climate and sufficient rainfall of about 40 inches per year, the Bronx River Valley possessed in the seventeenth century at the time of the European arrival a diverse and manifold flora and fauna. The richness of the area had attracted hunter/gathering Native Americans into the Valley some 8,000 years ago. Archeological digs have informed students that the first permanent settlements in the region began in the thirteenth century. Until the end of the seventeenth century some of these Native Americans tribes continued to reside in the Valley.

The Bronx River served as a borderline of the hunting grounds of local Native Americans: the Weckquasgeek on the west side and the Siwanoy on the east side, two sub—tribes of the Algonquin—speaking Wappinger Confederation. The Native Americans called the river Aquahung, meaning high bluffs, because of the gorges in the area of what is now the Borough of the Bronx of the City of New York. The most beautiful of these gorges can be found in Bronx Park, especially the one below the famous Hemlock Forest within the confines of the Botanical Garden.

By the year 1600, the eve of the European arrival in the area, the entire Wappinger Confederation numbered only 5,000. According to some authorities the word Weckquasgeek means the territory of the birch bark. Archaeologists point out that the birch bark was used to make kettles for cooking. In addition, the products of the forests, plains and river were used to provide food, medicine, clothing and shelter. The numerous tulip trees of the area provided logs to make canoes. White oak trees were stripped of their bark and then boiled, thus producing a medicinal remedy for the relief of aches and pains. Syrup from the many sugar maple trees provided flavor for Native American food.[3] For the Native Americans the Bronx River area was one huge botanic garden, the forerunner of what is now The New York Botanical Garden.

In 1623 the Dutch settled on Manhattan Island and began trading with the Native Americans, including the Weckquasgeeks. The main interest of the Dutch was in the fur trade. Soon, however, the Europeans began to view the area along the Bronx River as attractive for settlement. Jonas Bronck, born in Sweden in 1600, was the first European to settle in the river valley, named Bronck's River after him. In 1639 he purchased 500 acres of land from the local Native Americans; but Bronck was dead by 1643, probably as a result of a clash with these original inhabitants.

At first the Dutch settlers tried to trade and live peacefully with the Native Americans. Troubles, however, were inevitable because the Native Americans were losing their long—held land and the fur bearing animals (beaver, otter, mink and wildcats) were becoming depleted. By the end of the seventeenth century both the Native American tribes and the fur bearing animals in the Bronx River Valley were extinct, thus marking a significant change in the area.[4]

Before and after the coming of the Europeans the Bronx River stood as a boundary line, first between groups of Native Americans and then between European settlements. With the coming of the English in 1664 the River served as a boundary line between European settlers. To the west were the English—created manors of Fordham, Morrisania and the huge Manor of the Philipse Family. By 1693 Philipsburg Manor contained 91,000 acres stretching from Spuyten Duyvil in the south to the Croton River in the north. To the east of the River were considerably smaller sections of farmland owned by a relatively few, scattered families. By about 1670 the first bridge was erected across the River, just north of the present New York Botanical Garden. Since the bridge was built near the land of a small farm owned by John Williams, it was called William's Bridge, and now, of course, Williamsbridge. The bridge became part of the Boston Post Road and assisted the owners of small farms to the east of the Bronx River to transport their produce to markets on Manhattan Island.[5]

In the 1660s there were very few settlers north of the mouth of the Bronx River. With the British take—over of the Colony in 1664 Europeans moved northward and began another phase of changing the Valley of the Bronx River. Enterprising individuals built mills to use the River for its waterpower. The waterpower generated at these mills was used to turn grain into flour, logs into usable lumber, sharpen the tools of farmers and craftsmen and convert raw tobacco into snuff. The latter industry developed on what is now The New York Botanical Garden for here is located perhaps the most advantageous section for the harnessing of water power—the Great Gorge and the Falls of the Bronx River.[6]

The family associated with this enterprise at the Great Gorge was Lorillard, a name down to the present time identified with the tobacco industry and also with the botanical garden that was established in this section of New York City.[7] The origin of the Lorillard family can be traced to the town of Montpelier in the Herault district of France. Because the family members were Huguenot, they were persecuted in France. After settling for a time in the Netherlands, a country more tolerant of religious dissidents, some of the Lorillards came to the New World.

The founder of the New York branch of the family was Pierre Lorillard. The records do not indicate when he settled in New York City, but by 1760 Lorillard had completed an apprenticeship in the snuff—making industry, had started his own manufacturing business and was distributing snuff from an outlet store on Chatham Street in lower Manhattan Island. Producing different and popular types, his snuff business prospered. It is also related that some of his tobacco may have originated on the Virginia plantation owned by George Washington.

Pierre married Ann Catharine Mohr; and from this union there were born five children, two of whom, George (1766—?) and Peter (1768—1743), joined the snuff manufacturing firm and a third, Jacob (1774—1838), achieved great success in the tannery business that was centered on lower Manhattan Island. Because of Pierre's strong patriot sentiments, the family was forced during the American

Revolution to vacate their home in the British—controlled New York City. The family took up residence outside the City at the home of Pierre's parents, where he continued to express his support for American independence. The expression of these feelings eventually led to his death at the hands of Hessian soldiers. In 1882 P. Lorillard, a descendant, referred to the affair as "murder".

Pierre's wife managed the business until George and Peter were able to accept the responsibility. By 1792 the Lorillard tobacco company had become so successful that the brothers decided, in order to expand the business, to move the manufacturing portion outside the City. While maintaining the retail store in lower Manhattan, their manufacturing facilities were moved to the Bronx, which at that time was part of Westchester County. This move made them even more successful and enabled them to become enormously wealthy.

The location chosen by Peter and George Lorillard for a snuff mill is now the site of the New York Botanical Garden. At this spot the Bronx River, flowing through a one hundred foot gorge, is also enveloped by an extraordinarily picturesque hemlock forest. Before the American Revolution the value of this spot had been recognized with the construction of a dam and a wooden snuff mill. The Lorillards first purchased 50 acres of property along the Bronx River on September 24, 1792, from Richard and Mary Hunt of the Town of Westchester. Until 1870 (when the Family moved the tobacco business to New Jersey) the Lorillards continued to purchase additional real estate that eventually reached the total of 661 acres along the Bronx River.

By the early 1840s the Lorillards' business had outgrown the small, wooden, snuff mill that had originally attracted them to the area. It was replaced sometime in the early 1840s by a larger mill of native stone with brick trim. Constructed with wooden beams hewn from local trees and fashioned in lumber mills in the nearby Town of West Farms, it still stands on the eastern side of the Bronx River and is known as the Snuff Mill Restaurant of the Botanical Garden. A narrow canal (now filled—in and used as a roadway) was dug to divert the water that was needed to rotate the grinding stones of the mill. The Bronx River always supplied enough water and power; a minimum of 11.5 million gallons of water flowed down the gorge every 12 hours, even during the famous drought of the summer of 1798.

In 1856 the Lorillard Family built a magnificent home of some forty—five rooms on a bluff overlooking the great gorge. The mansion remained a well—known New York landmark until its destruction by an accidental fire in April of 1923. Near the mansion a stable resembling a rural church was constructed for the family horses. The Lorillards also developed a rose garden, known as the "Acre of Roses," whose petals became famous as the flavor for snuff.

When the Lorillard tobacco business moved to New Jersey in 1870, the Family members left behind a proud legacy. They had been careful to preserve and even enhance the locality's natural beauty: the great gorge of the Bronx River; a splendid falls that has been characterized as a miniature Niagara; the varied plants of their great estate; and the famous Hemlock Forest depicted as one of the finest of its type in existence. The only buildings still standing that can be traced back to the Lorillards are the 1840s snuff mill (now used as a restaurant), the stable (now a building to store equipment), and the stone cottage that was used as living quarters for servants (now a private residence). The establishment of the New York Botanical Garden on the site of the Lorillard estate can, in no small measure, be traced to the great care this Family gave to the maintenance and development of their property, thus helping to preserve in the midst of the urban sprawl of New York City a haven of plant life, trees, river beauty and rock formations that remain today practically unmatched in any part of the world.

Chapter III: Foundation

Throughout the early part of the nineteenth century there were discussions about establishing a botanical garden in New York City. By 1877 prominent New Yorkers moved beyond talking about the need for a garden. The plans at this time called for the garden to be associated with the Museum of Natural History and located in Central Park. In April of 1877 the New York State Legislature granted to Samuel B. Ruggles, Roger L. Stuart, William E. Dodge and others a charter empowering them to establish a botanical garden in the City of New York. The founders estimated that $300,000 to $350,000 had to be raised, mostly by private donation. Although shares of stock were sold for $25 each, the venture ultimately did not materialize.[1]

In 1888 the question of a botanical garden for New York City once again received serious attention. A lengthy *New York Herald* supplementary article on November 26, 1888, began with the statement: "The fact that the great city does not possess a botanical garden is a disgrace to New York and a reflection upon the country at large. So say many lovers of flowers". Many people were then consulted and their reflections were presented in the article. Someone pointed out that many European cities already possessed great gardens, with perhaps the finest located in St. Petersburg, Russia. The article declared that the National Botanical Garden in Washington, D.C., and perhaps the garden in Cambridge, Massachusetts (associated with Harvard University), "are the only ones worth mentioning in this country". Those people consulted urged that the proposed garden should be funded by the government but free of political interference, management and control. In addition, an outstanding botanist and administrator must be given complete authority to operate the garden that should be associated with some local institution of higher learning. The proposed garden would be a place for people to enjoy the beauty associated with horticulture and also a place for students to study.[2]

On the following day, November 27, the *New York Herald* carried a lengthy article expressing the endorsement of the New York Park Commissioners for the proposed botanical garden. Mr. J. Hampden Robb, President of the Board of Park

Commissioners, wholeheartedly supported the plan. He saw no objection to the garden subsidized by the Park Commission of the City of New York and then placed under private management. In fact he was "anxious to have some properly qualified society manage the proposed botanical garden". Robb closed his comments with the following invitation:

> I shall be delighted to meet anybody who is interested in the establishment of a botanical garden; all suggestions are welcome and if any society is prepared to take the initiative I and the other members of the Park Board will be pleased to receive them and discuss the matter.[3]

Probably unknown to Mr. Robb an interested, very distinguished society, judging by its history and membership, had already considered the need for a botanical garden in the City of New York. At a meeting of the Torrey Botanical Club[4] on October 24, 1888, the need for a garden was discussed. At this meeting Elizabeth Gertrude Knight Britton (1858—1934), the wife of Nathaniel Lord Britton (1859—1934),[5] described to the Club the couple's visit to the Royal Botanic Gardens at Kew in England. Dr. Britton later described how in 1888 he and his wife were visiting Kew Gardens to study collections made in 1885 and 1886 in Bolivia by Dr. H. H. Rusby. At the time there was no satisfactory herbarium in the United States; hence the necessity of journeying to Kew to study Rusby's specimens. During the visit Mrs. Britton turned to her husband and declared: "Why couldn't we have something like this in New York?" After their return to New York Mrs. Britton then gave her now momentous description of the Royal Botanical Gardens; momentous because it played an important role in the founding of The New York Botanical Garden. At the next meeting of the Torrey Club, held on November 28, the two *New York Herald* articles were used as the basis of a discussion for a botanical garden. To give further consideration the following committee (called the Garden Committee) of very distinguished men was then selected: E. E. Stems, Chairman; Arthur Hollick, Secretary; Thomas Hogg; H. H. Rusby; T. F. Allen; N. L. Britton; J. S. Newberry; Addison Brown.[6]

On January 8, 1889, the Garden Committee made its report and presented to the members of the Torrey Club a pamphlet entitled "Torrey Botanical Club Appeal for a Public Botanic Garden in New York City". The four page "Appeal" commenced with the following statement:

> The accumulation of wealth and the growth of public spirit in this metropolis make it reasonably certain that we shall have, sooner or later, a public botanic garden of the highest class. The sole question at present seems to be whether we shall have it very shortly, or wait another generation for its establishment.

It later declared:

Strictly speaking, a garden of this sort is a scientific and educational institution, quite as much so as a library or a college, and for its
foundation and maintenance the public may properly look to the
sources from which so many of our universities and libraries have been
derived.

Further on the "Appeal" stated:

The uses of a botanic garden may be reckoned as of four sorts.
First and foremost is the purely scientific and educational use. Sub-
sidiary to this, but still of a marked degree of importance, are the
pharmaceutical and horticultural uses, and, lastly, the general use as a
place of agreeable resort for the public at large.

The authors of the "Appeal" firmly believed that "Such a garden as New
York might have would speedily become a Mecca for the botanists" throughout
the world if American plants were significantly represented. The proposed garden
should additionally offer courses of instruction to New Yorkers, thus giving "a
great and desirable impetus" to the study of a very important and profitable science. The layperson would not be neglected because "the remaining use of a
botanic garden, as a place of agreeable and profitable resort for the general public,
is by no means to be lightly estimated". The "Appeal" closed with the following
very prophetic sentiments:

These are modest affairs, remotely and inconspicuously situated;
but a botanic garden of the highest class, established in New York City
or its immediate neighborhood, would be placed at the best imaginable
point to win a lasting reputation for itself and its founder, both in this
country and abroad.[7]

At this time the size suggested for the proposed garden was relatively small.
The gardens at Kew were sixty seven acres; the needs of New York might be
satisfied by fifty acres, "but it is suggested that seventy—five acres would be
none too much for its ultimate highest development."[8] It is interesting to note at
this time that this "Appeal" in 1889 proved to be a remarkably accurate blueprint
of the New York Botanical Garden long before its development into the twentieth
century. The members of the Torrey Club approved the "Appeal" and ordered a
printing to be circulated among the general public.[9] The activities of the Torrey
Club did not end with the publication and circulation of the "Appeal". Chairman
Sterns of the Botanic Garden Committee reported at the February 5, 1889,
meeting that the New York City Parks Commission had promised that suitable
property would be offered for a garden—if within two years one million dollars

could be raised.[10]

The background of this offer dates to the early 1880s. John Mullaly, the City Commissioner of Parks related in a report that, despite considerable opposition, the New York State Legislature approved a law that added 3,840 acres of parkland North of the Harlem River to the City of New York. The bill went into effect with the signature of the governor on June 14, 1884. The plan of the authors of this bill was to provide opportunities for recreation and prosperity to New York City, "destined within the next half century to be first among the cities of the world in population and wealth, first in culture, magnificence and power". Mullaly pointed out that the City's population was currently increasing at about 200,000 per year. At this rate the number of people in New York City would reach 1,900,000 in 1890 and some 3,000,000 in the year 1900. It was imagined that even the 3,840 acres was not sufficient and that 6,000 acres should have been laid out. Mullaly was confident that this park land would help to alleviate the horrible conditions existing in the overcrowded tenement areas of the City "where the death rate is so largely in excess of that in other parts of the city"[11] A suitable portion of this park land was the site promised by the Commission to the Torrey Club for the development of a Botanic Garden for the City of New York.

The members of the Botanic Garden Committee were obviously highly motivated and committed to bring to fruition the Torrey Club's concept of a magnificent botanic garden for New York City. They moved quickly and were achieving significant results in a very short period of time. On February 23, 1889, *The American Art Journal* in a very aptly named article entitled "A Million—dollar Garden" described the plans that had already been discussed or set into motion. The site chosen for the Botanic Garden was the southern portion of Bronx Park, one of the three major parks acquired in 1884 by the City of New York, the other two being Van Cortlandt and Pelham Bay Parks. Bronx Park consisted of over 650 acres, part of which would be given to the proposed Botanic Garden. There would be ample public transportation because the Suburban Elevated Railroad would soon be completed and provide a station just a few minute's walk from the proposed main conservatory. Then there was a very startling statement that a very grand entrance way had already been accepted, designed by the architects, Brunner & Tryon. An arched carriageway was planned

> with square—topped side entrances, the whole crowned by a classic cornice. Medallion portraits of Dr. John Torrey and the late Prof. Asa Gray occupy the spandrels above the arch, and those of Linnaeus and Jussieu are to be placed in the centres of elaborately decorated panels above the side gateways.

Subscriptions, large and small, would be sought for the construction of the garden. Donors of $10,000 would be called Patrons or Patronesses; contributors of $50,000 would be known as Patrons—in—Perpetuity, and the greatest benefactor would be the Patron—in—Chief. The committee proposed that "if this last mentioned contribution should be of overwhelming magnitude," then the garden would almost surely bear the name of this munificent donor. The planned name, at that time, was the Bronx Botanic Garden. Since the institution was envisioned as a "people's Garden", small donations were encouraged from persons of all walks of life. The minimum amount was $30, the payment of which could be spread over three years in $10 installments, "thus enabling any citizen of public spirit, however moderate his means, to take a personal part in the furtherance of this magnificent enterprise".

The Torrey Botanical Club plan called for the establishment of a Botanic Garden that would be, five years after its inception, "not only the crown jewel of our metropolitan park system, but also the greatest popular scientific institution on this side of the Atlantic". The article concluded with quotations of praise from the *Tribune, Times, Sun, Boston Transcript, Telegram* and *Evening Sun.* Ex—Mayor Hewitt, C. A Dan, George William Curtis and Charles Pratt also strongly supported the project.[12]

Obviously affairs had moved very rapidly, perhaps too rapidly and not to the satisfaction of all members of the Torrey Club and the Botanic Garden Committee. Sterns' statements to the press were criticized as constituting his own views and not those of the Club and Committee. The Torrey Club favored the foundation of a modern, scientifically oriented botanical garden in New York City. Influential members of the Club, however, were not anxious for the organization to become heavily involved in the formation, development and administration of the Botanic Garden. Much of what had transpired seems to have been the private agenda and the personal tactics of E. E. Sterns. A quite startling development occurred at the March 12, 1889, meeting of the Torrey Club when Sterns offered his resignation from the Garden Committee and it was accepted. Then on March 24, 1889, J. S. Newberry resigned, with no reason given.[13] For the rest of 1889 and for much of 1890 there was little movement on the botanic garden project.

In late 1890 the project was revived by the Torrey Club with a reorganization of the Botanic Garden Committee. Judge Addison Brown was added and Nathaniel Lord Britton and Arthur Hollick assumed a very active role as executives for the Committee. Brown brought the eminence of a member of the bar, Britton that of an up—and—coming member of the academic community (as a member of the faculty of Columbia College) with a growing reputation in New York social circles. Hollick possessed the reputation of being reserved, even tempered, deliberate and meticulous. In December, 1890, Brown, accompanied by his close friend and former judge, Charles T. Daly (1816—1895), went before the Park Commissioners to request an extension of the two year deadline to raise the one million dollar endowment. The request was readily granted. In January, 1891, prominent women were added to the Garden Committee, at the behest of Mrs. Charles Daly and Mrs. N. L. Britton. The Garden Committee was now composed of determined, influential individuals, men and women, who were not eager for publicity but who would move the project forward, with as little fanfare as possible.[14]

The next step was the introduction of a bill into the New York State legislature to incorporate the new garden. The bill stated that $250,000 was the immediate sum to be raised. The raising of a one million dollar endowment was not set aside, but was relegated to a future date. The act was passed by the State Senate and Assembly and then signed into law by Governor Hill on April 28, 1891.[15] The incorporators were forty eight in number and included such famous names as: Andrew Carnegie (1835—1919), J. Pierpont Morgan (1837—1913), Cornelius Vanderbilt (1843—1899) and Nathaniel L. Britton. The corporation would be managed by a Board of Directors that had to include (ex officio) the president of Columbia College, the professors of botany, geology, and chemistry therein, the president of the Torrey Club, and the president of the Board of Education of New York City. New York City then reconfirmed its promise to donate 250 acres of property in Bronx Park and money for the construction of buildings, when the sum of $250,000 was collected.[16] The act stated that the name of the new corporation was "The New York Botanical Garden" and was founded

> for the purpose of establishing and maintaining a botanical garden and museum and arboretum therein, for the collection and culture of plants, flowers, shrubs and trees, the advancement of botanical science and knowledge, and the prosecution of original researches therein and in kindred subjects, for affording instruction in the same, for the prosecution and exhibition of ornamental and decorative horticulture and gardening, and for the entertainment, recreation and instruction of the people.[17]

Chapter IV: Early History

On May 12, 1891, in the parlors of the American Geographical Society the first meeting of The New York Botanical Garden was held, with Cornelius Vanderbilt presiding. A twenty—member Finance Committee, including John Pierpont Morgan, was established. In addition, a ten—member Committee on the Constitution, By—laws and Nominations was formed, which included Seth Low (1850—1916), President of Columbia University.[1]

On May 19, 1891, a meeting was called to form a committee of prominent women to assist in raising the $250,000. Judge Charles P. Daly addressed this meeting and his remarks were later printed and circulated under the heading: "Want of A Botanical Garden in New York". These comments by such a prominent individual and their subsequent publication gave significant impetus to the campaign. In his remarks Daly stressed: 1) the scientific and economic importance of a botanic garden and 2) its recreational value for all classes of citizens. He pointed out that almost every European country and many cities on that continent have botanical gardens. Yet in North America, with a population at that time of 89 million (60 million of which were in the United States), there is only one botanic garden of any importance, that in St. Louis. In addition, the judge pointed out that North American fields, forests, swamps and sandy places were dying for various reasons and their demise certainly could be reversed with the development of a botanical garden. As to the recreational value, Daly stressed the importance of a garden for the growing American laboring class, who constitute the majority of the community, "and whose contentment with their lot is of the highest importance to the maintenance of public order". This was especially important at that time, according to Judge Daly, when great social changes were taking place and clashes were developing between the working class and the capitalist. He pointed out the injustice that exists with the buildup "of colossal fortunes, and the keeping and transmitting them without doing any thing for the public welfare, or for the working classes, whose labor made the making of them possible". The anarchists at that time were advocating an appeal to force to rectify these injustices. Judge Daly called upon the wealthy to begin to alleviate these grievances with a willingness to give a part of their great wealth "to promote the welfare and add to the enjoyment of their less fortunate fellow—citizens. A great botanical garden in this large metropolis would accomplish a great deal in this way".[2]

Judge Addison Brown gave the first donation of $25,000; this was followed in December, 1891, with a subscription from Columbia College[3] for the same amount. Between May and December, 1891, however, there were no meetings and very little progress was made, except that the interested parties were holding private discussions and devising plans to continue the project. Affairs moved very slowly over the next few years because of objections to the very strong presence of Columbia College in the formation of the Garden. Suggestions were made to include seven other educational institutions in the project, this proposal coming mainly from the City College of New York. Nevertheless, by February, 1893, seven contributors had given to the project $25,000 each: Cornelius Vanderbilt, D. O. Mills, John D. Rockefeller, Andrew Carnegie, and J. Pierpont Morgan had added their names to Judge Brown and Columbia.[4]

On February 25, 1893, a general meeting of the corporation was requested by five incorporators who believed affairs were moving too slowly. Vanderbilt chaired the meeting and Britton was the secretary, the first time the latter took such a visible role in the Garden project. From this meeting onward Britton usually was the spokesman to the New York newspapers. Since the $250,000 endowment had not been reached by $25,000 donations, J. P. Morgan's proposal to seek subscriptions of $10,000 and $5,000 was accepted. Morgan reported to the *New York Tribune* that the Finance Committee was confident that the $250,000 goal would be reached. In fact, the Committee had set as a goal an additional $500,000, which, when added to the $500,000 contribution from the City of New York, would provide a $1,000,000 endowment to the Garden. Professor Britton then displayed a map of the beautiful, 750 acre Bronx Park, from which the Botanical Garden eventually would select 250 acres. The general consensus favored selecting land on both sides of the Bronx River, which at that point possessed spectacular scenery. The opinion of those present was that "this picturesque stream would run through the centre of the garden". Britton informed the *Tribune*:

> No city in the world can boast of such a beautiful and desirable site for a botanic garden as New York... The Bronx Park, although now so little known to New—Yorkers, is destined to be one of the most beautiful and popular of the public parks in the world.[5]

With such a prophetic vision, no wonder Nathaniel Lord Britton become the dominant figure in the foundation and development of the New York Botanical Garden.[6]

On June 18, 1895, the most important meeting of the Corporation, up to that time, took place in the office of President Seth Low of Columbia College. *The*

New York Tribune announced that the $250,000 required by the Act of Incorporation had been reached through donations by twenty—one individuals who were now willing to have their names made public, along with the amounts of their gifts, now that the subscription goal had been reached.[7] This subscription money would not be used for the construction of buildings or improving grounds, but the $500,000 from the City of New York was designated for such purposes. All subscription money received would be placed into an endowment, the interest going toward maintaining the garden. The scientific directors, a small committee, which included N. L. Britton, had visited Bronx Park the previous week and selected a 250 acre section for the garden grounds.[8]

The Commissioners of Public Parks on July 31, 1895, approved the site selected and officially appropriated to the Botanical Garden the 250 acres, indicated by precise boundaries. The Parks Board stipulated that the Hemlock Grove (Tsuga canadensis), that primeval treasure of the selected site, was to remain undisturbed in its original state. The Board also suggested the beginning of propagation in nurseries and the labeling of trees. The corporation accepted all these conditions and funds were appropriated by the Parks Board. In fact, the first accomplishment of The Garden Corporation was the labeling of the largest trees and the removal of dead trees.[9]

Through the *The New York Times* of August 18, 1895, N. L. Britton announced to the public that careful consideration had been given to the site chosen by the scientific committee. It was noticed that this section of the City's park system possessed the natural beauty and "special adaptability to the uses of a botanic garden. Its peculiar diversity of surface and soil make it capable of producing the largest variety of floral and arboreal growths within a limited area". No one, however, should assume that the garden corporation was taking possession of such choice land for its own use. Instead, the corporation had taken on the grave responsibility, under the direction of a number of scientific experts, "to making this particular section of the public domain useful and educational as well as merely attractive and enjoyable".[10] As soon as possible the corporation began to function as a very active botanical garden.

The Garden's first public lecture was given on the evening of December 17, 1895, at the American Museum of Natural History by Dr. Daniel Morris, Assistant Director of the Royal Gardens at Kew; his topic was quite appropriately entitled, "The Rise and Progress of the Royal Botanical Gardens at Kew, England". On January 9, 1896, Britton presented to the Scientific Directors a topographical survey map of the garden that had been started in August, 1895, by the now deceased Mr. A. H. Napier, C.M. and completed by John R Brinley, who served for many years as the Landscape Engineer of the grounds.

On January 12, Britton informed the Board of Managers that 2100 young trees and shrubs had been bought and planted in a temporary nursery by Samuel Kenshaw, the first chief gardener. Charles S. Sargent, a noted horticulturist and Director of the Arnold Arboretum in Massachusetts, donated 310 valuable trees and shrubs, as a sign of support for the new botanical garden in New York City. By early March, 1896, Columbia College had agreed to "loan" its fine herbarium collection. With the purchase of the mycological herbarium of J. B. Ellis of Newfield, New Jersey, the Botanical Garden possessed excellent facilities for research and teaching. At the same time the Scientific Directors announced the inauguration of a regular publication. On April 15, 1896, Volume 1, Number 1 of the *Bulletin of the New York* Botanical *Garden* was published and contained such documents as the "Act of Incorporation", the list of incorporators, the names of officers and managers, the text of the above—mentioned agreement with Columbia, a report on the activities of 1895 and a financial accounting dated January 13, 1896.[11]

From its inception the New York Botanical Garden was a joint, cooperative venture between New York City and the Corporation. The City provided the property, funds and the labor necessary for the buildings and for landscaping, while the Corporation managed the enterprise and developed the educational and scientific facilities. As soon as the $250,000 subscription fund had been reached and the Park Commission approved the transfer of the property, emphasis shifted toward developing the site as a botanical garden. The actual plans began to take shape in October, 1895, under the direction of Calvert Vaux, a skilled landscape designer who was also the architect for the Parks Department. His selection was a wise one because all plans needed the approval of the Parks Commissioners. Although Vaux's work had been cut short by his tragic death in November, 1895, his plans did set the model for the future evolution of the Garden.

The details of actually arranging the garden grounds now fell to Nathaniel Lord Britton whose appointment as Director—in—Chief was announced in the *New York Sun* on May 22, 1896.[12] Britton, whose knowledge of contemporary botanical gardens was quite keen, announced that the buildings and plantings would, as much as possible, follow the natural contours of the park. On this point he was convinced that the design of the plantings, driveways and buildings should not interfere with the natural features of the park and, in actuality, "that all the general natural features of the area have been found to lend themselves to artificial improvements without any loss of beauty or effect". All members of the Park Commission did not agree with Britton's design and an acrimonious debate broke out, eventually spilling over into the newspapers.[13] Some compromises[14] eventually were made; not everyone was satisfied, but by July, 1897, the controversy had ended. Soon after, planting and gardening were started and in December, 1897, ground was broken for the museum building.[15]

Plans for the design of the Museum Building had been initiated in March, 1896, when a competition for architects was announced. The corporation stipulated that the building's location would be on elevated ground about 1000 feet east of the Bedford Park Station (now the Botanical Garden Station) of the Harlem Division of the New York Central Railroad. From the proposals made by a number of respected architects, those proposed by Robert Gibson were accepted.

Gibson's design contained elements of Italian Renaissance architecture, a gentle dome and rounded windows. The building was designed to be about 308 feet long, by 50 feet wide, with allowance made for wings to be added at some future date. Gibson painstakingly complied with "the directive that the building be in harmony with the landscape". The wooded, hilly, undulating background was not to be overwhelmed by the building. Gibson's specifications called for the front columns to be white stone, which in a few months, by virtue of its composition, turns grayish, thus blending into the surrounding plant life.

The interior of the building comprised a basement lecture hall to accommodate 800. The basement also included a museum of fossil botany to illustrate the evolution of plant life. The main entrance was located on the first floor and faced southward. Here were located administrative offices and a grand stairway leading to the second floor. In addition, the main floor contained an economic botany exhibit that demonstrated to the public the use of plants for food, drugs and other necessities of life. The second floor was devoted to systematic botany, containing exhibits of all plant life ranging from the most simple (mosses and seaweed) to the most complex (shrubs and trees). The public was invited to view the exhibits (some through microscopes); "thus the second floor, like the first, was for the public's education and interest". The third floor was designed for scientific research and called for a herbarium, library, classroom space, study and storage areas, and laboratories. This area was open only to researchers, which at the time included scientists from throughout the world.[16] The museum building was occupied in stages as each part was completed. In 1900 the staff was able to move into the administrative offices and the remaining portions of the museum were opened as construction was completed.

Gibson's design called for a fountain at the bottom of the steps leading to the museum's main entrance. The Corporation's Board of Managers called for an open competition which was won by the Carl E. Tefft. The sculptor named his creation the "Fountain of Life" because the character of its forms depicted the "Struggle for Existence" and the "Survival of the Fittest". The fountain has changed somewhat but at the time it was described as follows. There were two bronze horses seen to be leaping into the water. On one horse there is a nude female; with one hand she was attempting to restrain the horse, while with the other she indicated a gleeful gesture. On the other horse was a young lad trying to reign in the beast with one hand while holding a fish by the tail with the other. The pool contained a merman and a mermaid, both alarmed at the approach of the unexpected, frenzied steeds; both were viewed as turning to elude the wild creatures. Behind the horses was a globe surmounted by a dolphin with a beautiful child on its back. The child symbolically held in its hands a ship's tiller designed in a most exquisite pattern. From beneath the statue water flowed successively into three separate fountains.[17]

By the Summer of 1900 the first phase of the construction of the Conservatory had been completed with numbers 1—5 and 11—13 open to the public; the rest by 1902. This phase of construction also included the circular central house, one hundred feet in diameter and ninety feet in height. When the Conservatory was completed there was a total of fifteen horticultural houses covering an area of about 45,000 square feet. The houses were constructed so that they surrounded a large courtyard that contained ponds and other interesting features. Heat came from a powerhouse that also supplied the needs of the museum.[18]

The New York Times edition of Sunday, August 19, 1900, provided for the public an excellent coverage of the then constructed conservatories. The main entrance takes a visitor into the great palm house, with the dome ninety feet above the floor. At the time there were a number of palms, including five recently donated by a Miss Helen Gould. The Gould palms had been collected in the West Indies and South America, were fifteen to twenty years old and had outgrown the donor's greenhouse. Another attraction of the palm house is a great rubber tree, at least ten feet high, the gift of a Mrs. Grace. The description of the plants in the remaining houses demonstrated a wide variety of tropical plants. Most, if not all, were gifts of specified benefactors of The Garden. In addition, the article explained that the exhibits and placement of plants were not permanent.

> The arrangement of all the plants is more or less temporary and all plans are made with elasticity. A big typical greenhouse must evolve and develop as the result of study, but in the meantime everything is as beautiful as possible.[19]

This became the norm as the years and the collection of plants developed.

By 1906 there were about 10,000 plants in the entire Conservatory. The houses were arranged and numbered consecutively beginning with the large, domed structure known as the palm house, number 1. Continuing westward and then around the ranges (surrounding the inner courtyard) the houses continued until the house just to the east of the palm house was reached, which was number 15. Houses 1 through 4, 7, 8, 10, 11 and 15, were devoted to tropical plants. The plants of houses 12, 13 and 14 contained specimens from the temperate zone. Houses 5 and 6 comprised plants from the desert regions, including cacti and century plants. Number 9 house was devoted to aquatics.[20]

Chapter V: Developments Down to the Depression

The New York Botanical Garden began as an idea, one very inspirational, in the minds of two very talented, energetic and determined individuals, Nathaniel Lord Britton and Elizabeth Knight Britton . The Garden was incorporated in 1891, began operation in 1895 and by 1900 the construction of the main buildings was completed or at least well along to completion. The narration of this institution's history, by the end of the twentieth century one of the leading botanical gardens in the world, is a fascinating story of development and growth, largely as a result of the inspiration, impetus and direction of the Brittons.

In November, 1900, Dr. Britton reported on a very rewarding, seven weeks' trip to Europe. In Germany, France, Switzerland, England and the Paris International Congress of Botanists (where he represented the Garden and the American government) he was able to meet influential people, inform them of the New York Botanical Garden and arrange for the purchase or exchange of valuable plant specimens and herbaria. A large collection of Siberian shrubs was purchased at the Paris Exposition. They had originally been planted in the City of St. Petersburg in Russia. At St. Ouen, France, he purchased from C. Simon a rare collection of cacti and succulents. Britton spent nearly a week in Berlin where he arranged for the exchange or some important herbarium specimens. Concerning Berlin he commented that this is "the most active botanical center in the world". At the Royal Botanic Garden at Kew he was impressed with the high standards still maintained at this institution. Sir William Thistleton Dyer, Director, donated to the Garden duplicate herbaria from the Kew collection. Britton promised to reciprocate the favor when a representative from Kew next visited New York. This was the first, nor would it be the last, exchange between these two botanical institutions, one very young and the other much older.[1]

In his annual report for the year 1900 Dr. Britton, as Secretary and Director—in—Chief, described the remarkable growth and the status of the Garden. The herbaceous garden contained about 2,300 different species. The fruticetum or shrub garden had been increased with the purchase of a valuable collection from Biltmore, North Carolina. The collection now had about 450 species, an increase of about 110 over the number in 1899. The fruticetum was now sufficiently representative of shrubs hardy for this area of the United States. Near the northern end of the park the willow collection in a marshy area had been increased. In all about 220 different species of trees were represented throughout the grounds. In the eight completed conservatories there were 8,833 potted plants representing some 1,800 species. Throughout the garden, in the conservatories and in the wild sections, the total number of plant species available for study was at that time about 5,400, not counting lichens, fungi and algae.

Britton's report on the herbarium and the library for the year 1900 was also very encouraging. Through donations, purchase and exchange the herbarium collection was increased by 48,895 specimens, including the valuable assortment of the late Dr. Thomas Morong. The Morong collection was received from Columbia University and was added to those already donated by that institution. This brought the number of mounted specimens in the herbarium to 650,000, including the excellent collection of the deceased Professor Torrey, which alone was valued at $175,000. In the library the Columbia University donation had been classified and shelved; 1,415 volumes had been added during 1900, bringing the total collection in the library (started in 1896) to 8,832 volumes.[2] During the year 1900 Dr. Britton also reported on the garden's financial status: membership was over 800 at $10 per year; the endowment had reached $300,000; and the New York City Parks Board was making all the necessary improvement on the property.[3] These finances might appear to be sufficient but they had to cover many expenses, such as the cost of expeditions, publications and salaries. Concerning financial affairs and the great progress made under N. L. Britton, E. D. Merrill later wrote: "One marvels at the early and rapid expansion of this new institution, particularly when one considers the paucity of financial support in the early critical years". [4]

Between 1897 and the early 1990s The New York Botanical Garden has funded, organized and conducted over one thousand botanical expeditions by staff personnel, students and close collaborators. The Garden concentrated on North, South and Central America and the West Indies. The story of these excursions is a history in itself and not intended to be part of the present monograph. A brief description of the first Garden expedition suffices to illustrate the scope, magnitude and fascination of this aspect of the institution's many and varied activities.

In the summer of 1897 Dr. Per Axel Rydberg, who later became curator of New York Botanical Garden's herbarium, led an expedition to the Yellowstone Park area of the State of Montana.[5] On this trip, funded by Mr. William E. Dodd, Rydberg was assisted by Ernst A. Bessey of the University of Nebraska. The collections made in Montana contained about 800 species and numbered over 20,000 specimens. The importance of this Garden expedition was best summed up in Rydberg's conclusion that prior to his expedition "the flora of the state of Montana was very little known and still less understood". Based upon his explorations into Montana, Dr. Rydberg was able to collect hitherto unknown flora and publish his findings in a number of scientific papers, thus substantially increasing the knowledge of plant life in this area of the United States.[6]

The New York Botanical Garden also was involved at this time in laboratory research to change and improve people's eating habits, health and life style. A researcher by the name of Alexander Anderson decided to resolve the question of the relationship between starch and its hygroscopic nature. This marked the beginning of puffed cereals. He began his experiment in the Spring of 1901 at Clemson University in South Carolina, but obtained no results at that time. In August, 1901, he moved to New York City and began work at Columbia University. With his interest in the hygroscopic element of various grains, Anderson was given the opportunity to use the laboratories of the recently established New York Botanical Garden. It was here in Bronx Park that he worked on his grain experiments throughout the winter of 1901—1902.

Anderson knew that starch was found in almost all plants, but he was particularly interested in the cereal grains: rice, wheat, corn, barley, maize and oats. He knew that starch is an important food element, but as it occurs in nature the starch granules are so closely packed together that they are only slowly influenced by chemicals, especially those enzymes found in the human digestive system. Starch granules become more acceptable and beneficial as a food source when they are broken up. Anderson experimented and saw that this began to occur when starch was warmed in water at a temperature of 55—60 degrees centigrade and then burst at 75—80 degrees centigrade. On the other hand in dry heat he knew that little or nothing happened to the starch granules.

Anderson realized that nearly all starch could be expanded by this process, which then increased the nutritive value of the food. In addition, he noted that the "products obtained are pleasant to the taste, and the process may be varied to produce a great variety of flavors with any given cereal". Lastly, the food material by this process is "absolutely sterilized and may be preserved or stored for long periods".

In 1904 at the St. Louis World's Fair, Anderson's "invention" was a big hit as the "food shot from guns", and bags of puffed rice sold like the popcorn of today. In 1905 puffed rice was put on the market as a breakfast cereal. In later research Anderson developed "crackels" made of wheat, and oats that were also put on the market by the Quaker Company, for whom the inventor later worked for thirty—five years.

All of these accomplishments, however, had their beginning and first successes in experiments made at The New York Botanical Garden. The Garden made available to Anderson the laboratory facilities and an experienced staff of researchers. Considerable attention was given to the young scientist during his Garden stay, so much so that Alexander P. Anderson later publicly acknowledged that Dr. N. L. Britton and Dr. D. T. MacDougal (Director of the Laboratories) gave great, personal encouragement to him and his work, in addition to placing laboratories, equipment and staff at his disposal.[7]

From the Garden's inception the administrators sought valuable additions to the library, especially works illustrating the history and development of botany. In

March, 1902, an important purchase was made in Berlin of some 1200 volumes, all published before 1800. They became a very welcome addition to the 12,000 books already in the Garden's library.[8] In September, 1902, the Botanical Garden purchased "one of the finest collections of old and rare works devoted to botany and kindred subjects known to be in existence". The gem of this collection was "De Virtutibus Herbarium", published in Latin in 1450, and known as the first study on herbs. The purchase of this 400 volume collection gave to the Garden an unbroken history of botany from the early part of the fifteenth to the late eighteenth century. When these extremely rare works were added to the existing holdings of the library, the institution's administration believed that the New York Botanical Garden was "in a position to offer facilities to botanical students second to none in the world".[9]

Such features as roadways, bridges, fencing and lakes, vital to the park, were constructed as the need arose during the early years of the Garden's development. On December 23, 1897, New York City made the first appropriation, $15,000, for road building. The first bridge was built over the Bronx River at the northern end of the Garden and was completed by the end of 1903. At this time there was constructed a total of eight bridges; perhaps the most interesting one was on Pelham Parkway over the Bronx River and dedicated to the Swedish botanist, Carolus Linnaeus, on May 23, 1907, the two hundredth anniversary of his birth. Necessary fencing of the park was launched in the Spring of 1908 and completed in 1913. In 1904 and 1905 the lakes east of the museum were developed by flooding the marshes in that locality, thus furnishing an area for aquatic plantings.[10] By 1902 the Botanical Garden's popularity with the public was growing and the Manhattan Railway Company offered to extend its elevated facility northward from the Fordham terminus of the line. The planned addition called for a terminal at the southwestern corner of the Botanical Garden. The offer was accepted by The Garden, which then constructed a public walkway that was financed by the railway company. Construction of the walkway began in the early Spring of 1902. The work was completed by the end of the year and the facility was immediately made available to the public.[11]

Dr. Britton, as Secretary and Director—in—Chief, in his annual "Report for 1905" mentioned the growing numbers of schools, organizations and individuals who were seeking assistance in their visits to the Botanical Garden. The institute welcomed these visits for they helped The Garden to fulfill its responsibility of instructing people about plants and their importance. The Director stated that, whenever possible, young assistants in the various departments were used as guides. Even Mr. Skinner, the foreman of the conservatories, gave generously of his time in this regard. This kind of service, however, took these people away from their work, which was their first obligation to the institute. With the increasing number of visitors it was obvious to Britton that the presence of official guides, whose sole responsibility was to escort people, was the solution to this matter.[12]

Britton in his "Report for the Year 1906" related that steps had been taken to remedy this organizational weakness. In March, 1906, the *Journal* contained a "Guide to the Conservatories" with photographs, prepared by the chief gardener, George V. Nash. A complete guide to the grounds, buildings and plant collections had also been prepared, which included a plan of the grounds and pictorial illustrations. It had first appeared in the Bulletin, but was re—printed with a hard cover and sold for twenty—five cents a copy. Britton also announced in his "Annual Report" that two aids had been specifically assigned to meet visitors and personally guide them through the grounds, with proper explanations on the various sections of the park. Notices were placed in the museum building announcing that guided tours were conducted every day, except Sunday, starting at three o'clock. A regular schedule was established as follows:

Monday: Hemlock Forest and Herbaceous Garden.
Tuesday: Pinetum.
Wednesday; Fruticetum and North Meadow.
Thursday: Deciduous Arboretum Nurseries, Propagating Houses.
Friday: Public Conservatories.
Saturday: Museum.[13]

This marked the beginning of the volunteer services of the docents, a system of service that has operated with such great success and acclaim down to the present time.

In 1906, to mark the tenth anniversary of the founding of the New York Botanical Garden, the administration offered a series of ten seminars that were open to the public, free of charge. The program opened on April 21, with a lecture by the internationally known Dutch botanist, Professor Hugo de Vries of Amsterdam. The remaining lectures were given by staff members and local botanists, concluding with Dr. Britton's talk on "The Exploration of the West Indies", an area where the Director and the Garden had devoted much attention. Every effort was made to accommodate the public; the lectures were given on Saturday afternoon at 4:30 and ended in time for the participants to catch the 5:32 train at the Bronx Park Station.[14]

A new feature of The Botanical Garden was announced in November of 1906 with the development of an economic patch, which meant plants of a practical value to the human race. The Garden staff had always desired an area devoted to such specimens, but more important considerations delayed its development. This economic plot became very useful for a children's program started the previous year. This school program, involving children from 10 to 12 years of age, had been started in April, 1905, and offered lectures and demonstrations on Tuesdays, Thursdays and Fridays during the Spring and Fall. During April and May of 1905 about 2300 students attended the lectures, under the supervision and direction of their teachers. Each session consisted of museum lectures on the basics of plant life, followed by practical presentations in the conservatories and grounds, where the economic patch, after its establishment in 1906, became especially popular with the children.[15]

On January 29, 1915, the Board of Estimate and Apportionment of the City of New York appropriated to the Botanical Garden an additional 140 acres of park land. This donation of undeveloped land was accepted by the Garden's Board of Managers on April 15, 1915. Both banks of the Bronx River from Pelham Parkway to Williamsbridge, excluding three small portions of land set aside for the use of the City's Park Department, now belonged to the Garden. This additional land increased the total acreage of the Garden corporation to almost 400 acres[16] and included the old Lorillard family mansion built in 1856. Development and improvement of the new property was aided in cooperation with the New York Association for Improving the Condition of the Poor. Each day this Association sent about twenty men who worked with the small force of trained laborers of The Garden. The Association paid the wages of the men, thus providing assistance to the unemployed and aiding in a most effective way the development of the new tract of Garden property.[17]

A noteworthy feature of the early history of The New York Botanical Garden was the development of various specialty gardens. The earliest groups of these plantings were the rose, the iris, the dahlia, the daffodil and the rock gardens. The first of these gardens was the one devoted to roses; in fact during the history of the institution there have been four different rose gardens. The first rose bed was established in April, 1913, and located near the eastern end of the main conservatory. It was only about 250 feet long by eight feet wide.[18] When New York City gave the Garden a further 140 acres of land in 1915 a new rose garden was one of the features planned for the additional property. The site selected was in a valley located just south of the old Lorillard Mansion. The space allocated for the new garden was about three hundred and fifty feet long and two hundred and fifty feet across at its widest point. Mrs. Beatrix Farrand, noted horticulturist and landscape designer, and Mr. John R. Brinley, Landscape Engineer for the Garden, were authorized to prepare plans for the new rose garden.[19] Funded by J. P. Morgan, Andrew Carnegie, and W. K. Vanderbilt, it opened in the Spring of 1918 and eventually contained some seven thousand plants of several hundred different varieties. Gradually, however, the Farrand Rose Garden, as it was called, was abandoned because of the many demands placed upon the very limited staff tending the grounds of the Botanical Garden.

The third rose garden was developed immediately north of the Enid A Haupt Conservatory and was named the Bechtel Rose Garden to honor the memory of the late Edwin De Turck Bechtel, a noted lawyer, author and active member of the Board of Managers of the New York Botanical Garden. He also was extremely active in horticultural circles and was especially remembered for his planting of over 200 varieties of roses at his estate in Mt. Kisco, Westchester County, New York. The Bechtel Rose Garden, planned by Umberto Innocenti and Richard K. Webel, was officially opened on June 8, 1972.[20]

The fourth rose garden was named after Peggy Rockefeller and funded with a one million dollar donation by David Rockefeller. It bears significant historic value to The Garden for it follows the design and was located at the site of the old Farrand Rose Garden. An added attraction of The Peggy Rockefeller Garden was that it was not intended to be a static garden. Roses that did not do well would be discarded and replaced by varieties that showed great promise. The purposes of the Rose Gardens, therefore, were for beauty and for the design and development of better cultivars.[21]

In 1915 a modest Iris Garden was begun. The impetus for expansion was provided in January, 1920, when the newly organized American Iris Society was invited to establish its headquarters at the New York Botanical Garden. With the combined efforts of the two institutions the Botanical Garden's collection of irises by 1923 had increased to 1050 varieties, "constituting probably the largest collection, in number of forms represented, ever brought together in one place in America". Professional growers were able to view the vigor of the various types and their adaptability to regions such as New York. For the casual visitor it meant the opportunity to view a tremendous display of beauty.[22]

In 1918 the dahlia collection was started just north of the station of the Harlem Division of the New York Central Railroad. Requests for donations of roots were mailed to the most reputable commercial growers in the eastern portion of the United States. Prize winners at the recent dahlia show conducted by the Horticultural Society of New York at the Botanical Garden were also asked for donations of roots. Not everyone responded, but enough donations were made to begin a more than adequate iris garden.[23]

A daffodil collection was started in 1924 through the interest of the Dutch Bulb Exporters Association and Mrs. Wheeler H. Peckham of the Advisory Council of the Garden. The Association donated 37,000 daffodil bulbs that were added to 10,000 selected by Mrs. Peckham for naturalization in this region. During the Fall Season of 1924 the planting bed was selected and the bulbs were planted under the supervision of Mrs. Peckham.[24]

When the Park Department of the City of New York decided in 1915 to donate the additional 140 acres of land, the Garden was able over the years to add to its horticultural features. In 1927 the decision was made to add a long—desired rock garden in the southern portion of the preserve. The northern slopes of a hill facing the Herbaceous Grounds geologically and botanically provided an ideal location for a rock garden. From the top of the hill a small stream was laid out through natural and artificial channels. The garden was planted with bayberry, bearberry, blue—eyed grass, forget—me—nots; as well as some rare native plants such the trailing arbutus. As much as possible the rock garden imitated those found in Europe, especially in Switzerland.[25]

In 1932 this rock garden was replaced by the Thompson Memorial Rock Garden, which has remained one of the gems of the New York Botanical Garden.[26] The Thompson Garden is located east of the Enid A. Haupt Conservatory, close to the hemlock forest and the Administration Building. Designed in the

1930s by Thomas H. Everett, a horticulturist specialist on the Garden staff, it was located in a natural valley flanked on both sides with rock outcroppings. Containing a waterfall and several pools, it possessed some of the most unusual and beautiful alpine flowers and plants from the American Rockies, the Himalaya Mountains, the European Alps, the Pyrenees on the border of Spain and France and other great mountain ranges of the world. By 1938 The Thompson Rock Garden contained over 2,000 species of plants.[27]

During World War I (1914—1918) the development of the Botanical Garden continued, but the institution did experience some burdens as a result of this great conflict. As early as the Fall of 1914 the Garden Library's acquisition of valuable, botanical literature from Europe was curtailed as a result of warfare on the high seas. With America's entrance into the "Great War" in April, 1917, experienced Garden personnel began to leave for service in the various branches of the armed forces or for employment in war factories. By the Fall of 1917 a serious fuel shortage had developed when suppliers were not able to deliver the normal complement of coal. On January 3, 1918, in order to save fuel, Dr. Britton ordered the closing of conservatory range #2; the plant collection of this facility was transferred to range #1. At the time of the transfer it was very cold (lower than 12 degrees Fahrenheit), the tender plants, therefore, were placed on wagons, covered with straw, wrapped in blankets and the roots mulched with manure; and thus they arrived safely at range # 1, which was about a mile away. For the next year and a half range #2 remained closed, only being partially re—opened in October, 1919.[28]

Although there were a number of burdens for the Botanical Garden, the institution employed its staff and expertise to advance the war effort of the United States. Dr. N. L. Britton took the lead among American scientists to find substitutes growing in the wild to replace food in short supply or to provide alternate sources when prices soared. He pointed out that "dandelion greens and old fashioned lamb's—quarters and dock—all good substitutes for cabbage and spinach are going to waste every year right around our very doors". Britton declared that America's enormous supply of blackberries and dewberries were going to waste. The canning of these berries could easily supply the needs of the American Expeditionary Force fighting in Europe. The acorn, according to the Director of the Botanical Garden, could be used as meal for the making of bread. The Germans were already using the acorn for bread. Although it was not as tasty as regular bread, the substitute was very nutritious. In conclusion, Dr. Britton declared that "When we come to think of our wilderness wealth we are staggered by our wanton waste".[29]

With the end of World War I The New York Botanical Garden cooperated with the Federal Board for Vocational Education to develop and provide a very valuable gardening program for convalescing soldiers and sailors. The program began on January 15, 1919, with class work in the scientific laboratories. The students had the use of the Garden Library for research and the grounds and ranges for practical experience. The former members of the armed forces were provided with the theory of horticulture and "practical experience in the propagation and care of plants and in the maintenance of gardens and grounds". Funding for the program was provided by the Federal Board and by the Botanical Garden through donations from members and patrons interested in such a worthwhile project.

At that time there were many, profitable job opportunities for men in a field of work that provided a pleasant, healthy environment. Commercial greenhouses, public works projects and parks, and private estates were all seeking well—trained horticulturists. The program provided by the Botanical Garden was thorough, lasted for two years, and at the end of which time participants who satisfactorily completed the course work received a certificate. The program directors at the New York Botanical Garden stressed that the men receiving the certificate were "not garden laborers, but trained gardeners".[30]

During the 1920s there were several important developments and events in the development of the Garden. On March 26, 1923, the famous Lorillard Family mansion was destroyed by a fire that had its origin in the chimney of the old building. When the members of the fire department arrived, their efforts were hampered by low water pressure. Excellent salvage work kept the loss below $100,000, with most of the damage in the upper two floors. Nineteen paintings on loan from the Metropolitan Museum of Art and valued at $20,000 were saved. The naturalist, Dr. Edmund Southwick, however, lost his life's work on the flora and fauna of the New York area. For thirty—three years until his retirement he had been the entomologist for the City of New York and currently was the custodian of the herbaceous rounds of the Botanical Garden. Dr. Southwick's collection of slides, negatives, books and pamphlets was valued at $30,000.[31]   As for the stately Lorillard Mansion the building was eventually deemed beyond repair and demolished.

In 1925 the Board of Managers announced plans to develop the Botanical Garden into a world center for research on plant life, as well increasing the number of botanical expeditions. Dr. Frederic S. Lee, President of the Board, secured the participation of Dr. Samuel F. Trelease, newly—appointed professor of botany at Columbia University, in the announced project. Trelease agreed to research the importance of such factors as root development, nutrition, fungi, bacteria and the fertility of soil on the development of plant life, especially trees. A growing concern among scientists was the effects of automobile fumes on trees and ultimately upon humans. Lee underscored the fact that fundamental problems of disease in living beings, including humans, "can probably be studied more readily in plants than in animals or men". The Botanical Garden with its myriad plant life and excellent research facilities was the ideal place to center such a research program. In order to accomplish this goal of improving all life on this planet the Board of Managers was planning to raise a $7,000,000 endowment to augment the research facilities of the Garden and to provide the funds for horticultural exhibits.[32]

Concern was mounting for the condition of the famous Hemlock Grove that William E. Dodge, one of the founders of the Garden, called "the most precious natural possession of the City of New York". In December, 1925, Dr. Britton announced that one hundred new trees had been planted to assist the natural reproduction of the hemlocks. The Garden staff believed that the trees were not reproducing at the same rate as in other hemlock forests in North America. Britton declared that this scientific experiment would be repeated in the following year and would be watched with great interest by the scientific community. This effort to save the Hemlock Grove for posterity was "a chief task of the Garden's expanding activity in scientific research"[33]

During the Summer of 1926 a world flower show was held at the Garden. Among the flowers presented at the exhibition were: tiger lilies from China, the Australian straw flower in various colors, the purple flowered Chinese delphinium, and an orange South African daisy; every continent was represented in this exhibition that was highly publicized and well attended.[34]

After several years of developmental work The Garden announced on August 28, 1926, the completion of the aquatic garden. Located northeast of the Hemlock Grove, two small lakes were surrounded by trees usually found in wet places. These trees included red maples, alders, willows, sour gums and sweet gums, white ash, white swamp birch and oak. An attractive contrast was created with the line offered by the drooping willows and the wide—spreading red maples with their thick trunks and the rigid erectness of the slim trunk of the tamarack. Each of the lakes was developed with a different characteristic. One called the "Green Arrow Pond" exhibited thick clumps of arrow arum, a plant that has deep, arrow—shaped leaves. The second, the "water Lily Lake", was developed with an open surface, except for a large patch of wild water lilies with white and pink blossoms.[35]

By the Fall of 1926 the complete results of an expedition to British Guiana in 1921 by Dr. H. A. Gleason, Curator of the Garden, were announced. Not only were the consequences of this venture extremely important, but the entire story was of great interest to the public. When Gleason completed his work in 1921 and was preparing to return to America, his guide, an Indian named La Cruz offered to continue gathering plants. Although somewhat skeptical, the Curator sold to La Cruz and another Indian, Mendonca, his entire outfit of collecting tools.

During the exploration the Indian guides certainly demonstrated their knowledge of the area for during the expedition they were able to give the native name of almost all plants and in many cases the curative value of certain specimens. A few months after returning to The Garden Dr. Gleason was informed by Customs that a box of plants awaited his claim. For the next three years various plants, which reached almost 30,000 in number, were sent by La Cruz and Mendonca to New York. By 1926 scores of hitherto, scientifically unknown specimens were in the possession of The New York Botanical Garden and eventually classified.[36]

In early 1927 it was announced that the Garden's museum building, the largest such structure in the world, would be equipped with electric lighting. Up until that time the massive, three—story building was equipped only with gas lighting. For most of its thirty years of existence this method of gas—lighting was sufficient. The building was open, almost exclusively during the day and the gas lighting was used only on dark days. Increasingly, however, experiments were conducted throughout the night and the gas lighting system proved to be inadequate. Arthur J. Corbett, superintendent of buildings and grounds, convinced the Board of Managers of the Garden to seek funds from the Board of Estimate of the City of New York to make the conversion. The Board of Estimate agreed; the cost was placed at almost $20,000 and the conversion took more than a month to complete.[37]

On January 15, 1928, Dr. John K. Small, Chief Curator of the Museum and Herbarium of the New York Botanical Garden, was granted a leave of absence to assist Thomas A. Edison (1847—1931) in his quest for alternate rubber sources in the southern portion of the United States, especially in Florida. In making the announcement Dr. Britton, Director—in—Chief, described Small as very knowledgeable in the vegetation of Florida, having conducted a number of expeditions to the area. Edison was seeking to find sources and methods of producing rubber in commercial quantities from plants native to Florida.[38] For some time Edison had been operating a very modest, limited search from his home in Ft. Myers, Florida. On the other hand, for the past thirty years Dr. Small had made annual trips to Florida and other southern states to study the flora of the area. During his trips he had discovered numerous plants previously unknown to horticulturists. The hope was that the combined expertise, experience and determination of these two scientists would produce new sources of rubber for which the demand was growing, especially with the increased use of the automobile.[39]

Thomas A Edison's interest for a new source of rubber had been increased in July of 1927 by a visit made to the New York Botanical Garden. On this visit, Dr. Small introduced Edison to the institution's 40,000 volume library, where he was surprised to find so many books on botany. Since then he had multiplied his efforts of reading, exploring and experimenting to find new sources of rubber.

Small spent six weeks with Edison and upon his return reported that Edison was prepared to spend ten years, if necessary, to find a plant that could yield 10 to 12 percent of rubber, was resistant to frost, and could satisfy the nation's need for one and one half million tons of rubber per year. In addition, Edison was seeking a plant that was capable producing rubber eighteen months after the planting of the seed.[40] Obviously, Thomas A Edison was not successful in his quest, for the great scientist passed away in 1931.

On June 7, 1929, the newspapers announced that Dr. Nathaniel Lloyd Britton, who had reached his seventieth birthday in January, had asked to be relieved of his positions and duties as Director and Secretary of the New York Botanical

Garden. With his contributions to the City of New York and to the scientific community too numerous to mention, *The New York Times* declared that

> During Dr. Britton's administration the garden has progressed from what was practically a wooded waste to a position where its botanical and horticultural exhibits are world—know. The number of exhibits runs into millions, as does the yearly attendance, the Sunday attendance alone averaging 50,000 persons.

From a wonderful idea, the institution had grown by 1929 to third place among the world's botanical gardens. In Britton's own words his motives for retirement were as follows:

> My primary reason for desiring to resign from my duties with the Botanical Garden is to devote myself more thoroughly to private research. I have no special subjects in mind, other than a general interest in the vegetation of tropical America. There is a fertile field available in the detail of vegetation in Puerto Rico and the Virgin Islands.[41]

Chapter VI: The Depression Years

On July 21, 1929, The New York Botanical Garden announced that Dr. Elmer D. Merrill was chosen to succeed Dr. Britton as Secretary/Director of the institution. He agreed to take office on January 1, 1930; meanwhile Dr. Marshall A Howe served as Acting Director. Merrill, age fifty—two, came to the Garden with a distinguished record in teaching, administration and research in the United States and abroad. At one time he was Director of the Bureau of Science and Professor of Botany at the University of the Philippines, where he concentrated on surveying the flora of the Indo—Malayan regions. Before accepting the appointment at The Garden, Dr. Merrill had served since 1925 as the Dean of the College of Agriculture at the University of California.[1] During Merrill tenure (1930—1935) the Garden would engage itself in many public service activities.

During the Summer of 1929 hay fever was especially rampant in the Bronx and surrounding areas. Fittingly The Garden, under the direction of Dr. R. P. Wodehouse, had been conducting research on the structure of the pollen that caused such misery for so many sufferers of hay fever. There was on display twenty different types of pollen that were the culprits causing the allergic reaction. Wodehouse pointed out that the tiny, one—celled grains were invisible to the naked eye, but could be seen under the Garden's powerful microscope that magnified the pollen to two hundred times its actual size. Not only was The Garden hoping through its research to aid sufferers, but it also had invited the public to view the pollen under the microscope; and many individuals took advantage of the invitation. At that time immunization required at least twelve to sixteen, painless injections for treatment. The Garden was searching for a far simpler procedure.[2]

As a service to the public in its teaching capacity The Botanical Garden in late 1929 had on display a collection of antique and obsolete microscopes. Of particular interest was a horizontal microscope, believed to be the only one of its kind in existence at that time. This valuable, ancient microscope was presented to the Garden by Mr. L. London, a Bronx collector and dealer in old and new scientific instruments for the past thirty—eight years. This microscope was of enormous size, nearly six feet long, but only had magnification equal to an ordinary reading glass; whereas compact microscopes at that time could magnify several thousand diameters. Its value, of course, rested in its uniqueness and antiquity. In his curiosity Mr. London researched the history of microscopes and found that a similar one had been produced in Europe in 1693 by a craftsman named Bonnani. Mr. London, however, through further study had determined that his instrument was far more crude than Bonnani's and thus assumed that it must have predated the latter's microscope.[3]

In August, 1930, Elmer D. Merrill, The Botanical Garden's newly appointed Director, attended the Fifth International Botanical Congress that was held in Cambridge, Great Britain. The Director, along with four colleagues from The Garden, joined more than 2,000 delegates from fifty—four different nations. In recognition of his stature among botanists Merrill was chosen to chair all sessions of this most prestigious international gathering. He was also chosen to chair the ongoing work of the most important sub—committee——the group delegated to arrive at a standardized flower nomenclature for the entire world. Dr. Menill pointed out that there was a wide difference in the names used for plants among botanists throughout the world. Add this to the great variety of languages, and it is easy to understand the differences of opinion and usage in regard to nomencla-ture. In spite of these very evident problems Dr. Merrill believed that his com-mittee would make progress because of the very evident spirit of co—operation that was present during the conference sessions held August 16 to 20, 1930.[4]

Dr. Menill's 1930 "Annual Report" as Secretary and Director reflected in a serious manner the economic crisis facing the nation and the world as a result of the Crash of 1929 and the resulting Great Depression of the 1930s. He reported:

> At present the institution is a static one; in fact, because of essen-tial salary adjustments made in 1930, all other items have been so dangerously reduced, that unless additional resources become avail-able within a few years, reduction in activities and reduction in staff will be inevitable.

In particular, he called attention to the serious fire hazard that existed in the Museum Building. The structure itself was fireproof, but its contents, such as the contents of the library or storage areas, were highly inflammable. If a fire oc-curred on the upper two floors, the conflagration could easily get out of control and the valuable and irreplaceable library and reference contents would be de-stroyed.

On the other hand the problem of inadequate staffing had been somewhat alleviated by relief programs organized by the federal government in its efforts to assist those individuals unemployed as a result of the great depression that started in 1929. The Emergency Work Bureau provided women for indoor work and men to work on the grounds; and then paid the wages of these employees. Merrill reported that during the year 1930, as a result of the assistance of this federal agency, a substantial amount of delayed work and maintenance had been completed and new projects initiated.[5]

On the grounds one hundred and seventy—nine men, up to eighty at a time, were employed at manual labor. The work consisted of grading, constructing paths, painting, clearing tracts of land, removing dead trees and shrub and preparing the land for planting. The women were mainly utilized in the herbarium where The Botanical Garden had fallen many years behind (in some cases specimens had been in storage for twenty—five years) in the work of preparing and mounting dried plants on sheets of paper, providing the proper names, getting them classified and finally arranging them in the permanent collection. This type of work required skilled assistants, women with a good education; for the most part The Emergency Work Bureau was able to supply these qualified women. Two of the most talented were linguists who were more or less fluent in seven languages. The linguists were able to translate and record information on specimens that had been stored for years for the lack of such competence. Others did stenography, filing, cutting, mounting and even some microscopic examinations. Dr. Merrill reported: "Normally we mount 12,000 specimens a year. Now we are running to 100,000. This material is fundamental to research and of interest to all who grow crops or any plants".[6]

The income of The Botanical Garden, however, continued to decline during the early years of the Great Depression. For 1932 there was a reduction in income of $90,000 from that of 1931; this represented a 20% decline. For 1933 there was a reduction of $74,000 from that of 1932; this represented a 17% decline. In addition, the City of New York reduced its contribution by $13,230 for 1934; and further reductions from the City were expected. The Director called upon all persons associated with The Garden to render wholehearted and harmonious support in all their endeavors at the institution.[7]

Without the assistance of the various federal relief agencies the activities of The Garden were seriously threatened. Both Dr. Merrill and his successor Dr. Marshall A. Howe, who became Director of the Garden in the Summer of 1935,[8] acknowledged the vital assistance rendered in diverse areas, especially in finances. Howe signaled out for special recognition and gratitude the assistance, in the form of wages and material, of the Works Progress Administration (WPA) and its predecessor, the Public Works Administration (PWA). For 1934 the total financial relief received from federal agencies amounted to $180,000. For 1935 the final amount had not been reckoned by the time Director Howe had issued his "Annual Report", but he estimated federal funding at between $200,000 and $250,000.[9] This government assistance continued, more or less, into 1941 when the nation's economy began to revive as America initiated aid for the Allied World War II effort.[10]

In the early 1930s there was a growing desire at The New York Botanical Garden to inaugurate a school for professional gardeners——similar to that conducted at the botanical gardens at Kew and Edinburgh in Great Britain. The original intention was to provide a scientific course of study for the younger members of the staff. During the day they would work at their gardening duties and in the evening take courses in a specific program of class study. The number of participants would be limited; new students from the staff would be admitted as vacancies occurred. Admittance into the program would be based upon the practical experience previously gained in the gardening profession. When knowledge of the proposed program became known, gardeners on local estates requested admittance. To make the greatest use of this unique program, the first of its kind in the United States, fifty—eight participants were admitted into the first program. The basic requirement was at least four years of practical gardening experience. A program originally intended exclusively for Garden personnel was thus made available to area gardeners and horticulturists. The courses were scientific in content and were offered on Monday and Wednesday evenings during the Fall and Winter months. Designed to give the experienced, professional gardeners a sound grounding in the sciences the following course of studies was offered.

First Year: Systematic Botany, 12 lectures.
          Plant Morphology: 12 lectures.
          Physics and Chemistry, 12 lectures.
          Plant Physiology, 12 lectures.
Second year: Soils and Nutrition, 12 lectures.
          Entomology, 12 lectures.
          Plant Pathology, 12 lectures.
          Plant Breeding, 12 lectures.[11]

Over the first two years some sixty—five people attended, not all of whom sought the certificate awarded to those who successfully completed the program. Participants included people from New Jersey, Westchester County, Long Island and one person from Albany, New York, the latter forced to travel some one hundred and fifty miles each week after a change in jobs took him to that City. On the evening of April 9, 1934, twelve gardeners received their certificates for successfully completing the program in the First American School for Professional Gardeners. The Botanical Garden program was judged a huge success because it

> emphasized the nobility and satisfaction of the gardening profession, the value of basic technical knowledge in making any plantsman a helpful influence in his community and the benefits that were certain to be derived by all participating individuals and institutions as well as the entire horticultural field .[12]

In 1938 a two—part program of horticultural studies was organized for the amateur gardener or someone with no gardening experience. The first course, "Introduction to Gardening", consisted of eight evening lectures of one hour in length; a fee of $8 was charged to the participants. The topics covered were: The perennial border, its preparation and management; Annuals and their culture; Roses; Summer bulbs and tubers and their uses; Hardy shrubs; Lawns; Vegetative propagation; and Rock gardens. The second course, "Gardening Practice for the Home Grounds", was offered on Wednesday afternoon, with the lectures repeated on Saturday afternoon. The fee for participants was $15. There were ten meetings consisting of one hour of lecture and one and a half hours of practical demonstration. The ten topics offered were: Preparing the ground for planting; Pruning; Lawn making and maintenance; Planting; Seed sowing and raising of young plants; Potting and repotting; Disease and pest control; Vegetative propagation; Cold frames and hotbeds; and Maintenance of ornamental plantings. No prior knowledge or experience in gardening was necessary, nor was the introductory program a prerequisite for the gardening practice program.[13]

A very interesting public service program was offered by The Garden, beginning in February, 1940. It centered on the identification of plants in the New York area. This program was designed especially for New York City teachers to aid them in their class presentations. It was also open to scout leaders and those individuals interested in nature studies. Meeting on nine Saturdays between February 3, and June 8, the program comprised a total of thirty hours of work. During the winter months attention was given to lichens, mosses, and evergreens. During the Spring, flowering plants were studied, with several all—day field trips included. The cost for participants was $10, but only $5 for teachers, whose administrators at the Department of Education were informed of their participation in this enrichment program.[14]

The New York Botanical Garden reached a great milestone in its history and development when the two millionth specimen was added to its herbarium. The occasion was marked by a special ceremony attended by one hundred invited guests on the afternoon of Wednesday, December 11, 1940. The milestone was reached when Mr. Joseph R. Swan, President of the Board of Managers, placed a very rare specimen of Clematic versicolor in it proper place in the herbarium. This species had added significance because it was initially introduced to science in 1901 by Dr. John K. Small, Curator and for forty years a member of the staff of the New York Botanical Garden. The herbarium had its beginning in 1896 and had grown at a remarkable rate. On the average the herbarium specimens had increased at the rate of about 40,000 each year. By the end January, 1941, when the *Journal* account describing the milestone event was published, the herbarium had added another 19,000 specimens. By that time it contained 1,383,833 specimens of flowering plants and ferns; approximately 177,000 mosses; 61,400 liverworts; 87,500 algae; and nearly 305,000 fungi, including lichens, for a grand total of 2,019,000. The Garden herbarium at that time was first in plants from certain regions such as the southeastern portions of the United States, the West Indies and Bolivia and in the flora of Asia. In his concluding remarks on the history of the Garden herbarium John Hendley Barnhart, a long—time member of the staff, commented:

The combined herbaria now contain two million specimens. This is true of no other herbarium in America, and not more than five or six in the Old World. In certain departments, as in flowering plants and in fungi, there are two or three larger accumulations in this country. On the other hand, in some fields, as the mosses, it is believed that there is no collection as large anywhere in the world.[15]

Chapter VII: World War II

With America's entrance into World War II, following Japan's attack upon Pearl Harbor on December 7, 1941, The New York Botanical Garden immediately made plans to contribute to the war effort. In an editorial in the *Journal* of January, 1942, Secretary/Director William J. Robbins (1937—1957) mentioned the great conflict's impact upon The Garden and outlined, in a very general manner, the ways The Garden proposed to support America's war effort.

Robbins mentioned that by January, 1942, fifteen Garden men had become part of the United States Armed Forces, this represented a 14% reduction in staff and undoubtedly marked only the beginning of the loss of experienced garden employees.[1] In addition, fifty had volunteered and had been accepted as air raid wardens, while others began training to become nurses' aids in the Red Cross and similar organizations.

Most importantly Secretary Robbins mentioned that every institution had to contribute to the war effort, but that a botanical garden, by its very special nature and mission, could make very unique contributions. In the first place, combat had interrupted the production and transportation of essential materials, especially those from distant lands and vitally connected with the war effort. With The Botanical Garden's extensive knowledge, excellent staff and unusual plant collections, every effort was made to seek and provide substitutes for those materials in short supply.

Secondly, The Garden, with its magnificent setting and beautiful plants, shrubs and trees had always been an attraction in providing relaxation from the arduous duties of life. The Botanical Garden promised to make every effort to sustain and nourish the morale of all those who visited its spectacular parkland.

Lastly, those at The Garden realized the importance of food in the war effort. Plans had already been established to provide special programs in the cultivation of vegetables. Designed by the most informed horticulturists, these programs were fashioned to provide participants with a sound understanding of land conservation, fertilization, planting, caring and harvesting of the crops that provide an abundant yield of nutritious food. In conclusion W. J. Robbins assured the public that "We have confidence in the future and will continue to serve individually and as an institution in any way we can".[2]

In the January, 1942, edition of the *Journal* The Garden immediately published an article entitled "Practical Vegetable Growing For Amateur Gardeners". The author, James S. Jack, provided practical and understandable tips on growing a successful vegetable garden. His suggestions, with ample explanations, included:

1. Choose a sunny spot for a vegetable garden.
2. Prepare the ground thoroughly, preferably in the Fall.
3. Buy your seeds (also fertilizers) only from reliable dealers.
4. Buy young plants from places where they are grown.
5. Plan for periodic sowing of seeds to insure supplies of fresh young vegetables throughout the season.
6. At the end of each row place a label giving the date of sowing and the name of the variety.
7. Keep the ground well cultivated.
8. Keep weeds under control.
9. Use rotenone against insect pests.
10. In the Fall, clean up the vegetable garden and turn the soil so that it will pass the winter in a rough condition.

The author urged families to set aside a sizable plot, 50 X 100 feet (even a smaller garden served a useful objective) was sufficient to provide a family of four to six with ample vegetables throughout the growing season. James S. Jack believed that those families, who immediately started to plan in January and acted properly when the growing season arrived, were guaranteed "an abundance of nutritious food of the finest quality for many months".[3]

On January 28, 1942, The New York Botanical Garden and *The New York Times* began a six week, co—sponsored series of lectures entitled "Vegetable Growing for Victory". There were four hundred people in attendance at the first meeting, with five hundred applications rejected because of the limited capacity of the *New York Times* Hall at 240 West Forty—fourth Street. The same program was repeated twice each Wednesday until March 4. F. F. Rockwell, garden editor of *The New York Times*, presided, with T. H. Everett of the Botanical Garden presenting most of the lectures. All the basics of gardening were mentioned with special emphasis on the importance of sun, fertile soil, a level plot of ground, good drainage and suggestions of crops that are easily grown. Participants were urged to start slowly and to delay planting corn, peas and Brussels sprouts until they had gained enough experience. In closing remarks E. L. D. Seymour of the National Garden Advisory Committee urged: "The important thing is that food shall be grown, that it be grown well and handled carefully and that there shall be no waste".[4]

Starting in September, 1942, The New York Botanical Garden and *The New York Times* again co—operated in a program of four lectures for those who developed Victory Gardens in the Summer of 1942. The purpose of this series was to present suggestions for these gardeners to reap the greatest advantages from their summer efforts. The topics covered in the four part series of the program were: canning and storing of home—grown vegetables and fruits; getting the garden ready for next season; and producing fruit in the home garden. The lectures were given on Wednesday evening at 8 P.M. and once again given in *The Times* lecture hall on West 44th Street in Manhattan. There was no admission charge, but, because of limited space, tickets were required and available by writing to the Garden Editor of *The New York Times*.[5] The two series of lectures were attended by nearly fifteen hundred people. Early in 1943, to reach as many segments of the population as possible, assorted locations and various means of communication were implemented by the New York Botanical Garden to encourage and instruct the public on proper gardening techniques. The department store R H. Macy and Company requested that the Garden conduct a six week course in Victory Vegetable Gardening in a small auditorium on the fifth floor of its location at 34th Street and Broadway. Lecturers were drawn from the Educational Program of The Garden. Presentations on the basics of gardening were given daily at 11 AM. and 2:30 P.M. and on Thursday evening. Actual planting demonstrations were given on the stage of the auditorium, followed by a question and answer session.

On March 28, 1943, The Garden began a five week free lectures series, held on the grounds each Sunday afternoon. The program was conducted in conjunction with the Civilian Defense Volunteer Office of the Bronx and consisted of lectures followed by outdoor demonstrations by various members of the staff. The program called for the lecture to be based on the gardening activities to be accomplished during the coming week.

To reach the public on the importance of wartime gardening The Botanical Garden also made use of the media of radio broadcasting. Time was made available by Station WNYC, the Municipal Broadcasting System. On each Monday evening from 6 to 6:15 starting on March 22, and concluding on April 12, there was a question and answer program. Garden staff members were available to supply answers to the various problems confronting Victory Gardeners. Each Friday afternoon various members of the Anti—Aircraft Artillery Command of the New York Region traveled to The New York Botanical Garden to learn how Victory Gardens could be developed at the various bases in the area. On March 29, 30, and 31 and again on April 26, 27, 28, "Three—Day Short Courses in Practical Gardening" were given on the grounds. Staff lectures and demonstrations were part of the programs.[6]

The New York Botanical Garden quite naturally became involved in overcoming wartime shortages of plant matter. A very serious shortage of quinine had developed when Japan occupied Java. This island in the Far East was the only place where the cinchona tree, from whose bark quinine was made, was grown commercially. With many of the armed forces of the United States serving in the tropics and thus exposed to malaria, a shortage of quinine was indeed a serious matter. Members of the Garden staff instructed field employees of the Office of Economic Warfare (OEW) to recognize the cinchona tree in the wild. Thus instructed, these workers combed the jungles of Central and South America for groves of cinchona trees and employed locals to harvest the bark from which quinine was then extracted.

The occupation of the Philippine Islands by Japan early in the war created a serious shortage of heavy—duty rope. The Philippines had largely provided the United States with America's supply of hemp. The Garden was able to point the American government in the direction of an alternate source. The ancient Aztecs of the Yucatan Peninsula had devised a system of making rope from the fiber contained in certain pineapple plants growing in that region of Mexico.

At that time castor oil was the best—known lubricant for the engines of propeller—driven airplanes. Researchers at The Garden provided the necessary information for the government to select the best castor bean; a bean that yielded both the finest and the greatest amount of oil. Members of The Garden staff were able to provide a Virginia plantation owner with proper information on growing pyrethrum, which was an essential ingredient for producing safe domestic insecticides. Before the beginning of World War II pyrethrum was easily obtained from British East Africa. Now this source was almost completely denied to the United States by the war at sea.

The United States Army also profited by information supplied by The Garden staff. Army units that needed camouflage material for concealment and material to build earthworks were provided with information on the fastest—growing and most durable grasses and plant life. The military at that time was misinformed about the primrose plant; that it was poisonous with a reaction similar to poison ivy. The Botanical Garden personnel was able first "to assure the Army that the domestic primrose is as harmless as a buttercup" and second that the Asian variety was poisonous; therefore, soldiers in that theater of the war were instructed to recognize the plant and to avoid it.[7]

Relying on its extensive experience, The Garden provided a program to train botanists for work in tropical areas. From its vast store of knowledge on plant life Garden researchers also provided the government with information on the means to obtain alternate supplies of rubber, on the medicinal value of various drugs, on the uses of various fibers and on the edibility of tropical plants. A serious problem facing the United States Air Force was that the wiring of airplanes was being short circuited, especially in the tropics. Research at The New York Botanical Garden provided the information that the cause was fungi which has "a disposition to cause short circuits"[8]

During the War the United States Navy was faced with the chore of getting various types of timber out of the Amazon region. The question was the specific gravity of the wood in which the navy was interested. If it was heavier than water, then a railroad would have to be built to haul out the logs. The Navy was able to find the answer to various timber problems in the excellent library of The New

York Botanical Garden. During World War II soldiers in the tropics were plagued by the fungus, Trichophyton mentapophytes, which caused the debilitating ailment, commonly known as athlete's foot. During the War and into the early 1950s The Garden investigated the fungus for the Army and for the general public.[9]

In March, 1945, The Garden, at the request of the Bronx County Red Cross War Fund, helped the war effort in a rather unique manner. It constructed a display in conservatory #4 to publicize the role played by the Red Cross during World War II. The display consisted of two jungle huts——one a typical recreation center and the other a medical unit. Both were recreations of what was available to United States servicemen, through the Red Cross, in a jungle area, presumably in the Philippines. The recreation center, the larger of the two huts, contained such items as a phonograph, writing desks and benches. Conservatory #4 also had been converted by the Garden into a jungle setting with plants native to the Philippine Islands.

On Sunday, March 4, when the display opened, various dignitaries attended and gave brief addresses. Undoubtedly the most interesting personage was a Lieutenant Colonel Benvenuto Dino, a native of the Philippines currently attached to the plastic surgery staff of the Columbia—Presbyterian Medical Center in New York City. He gave an "enthralling account" of the wonderful work of the Red Cross throughout the war in his native Philippine Islands. Even during the long occupation of the Islands by Japan the Red Cross provided, under great stress and with enormous difficulty, vital assistance to the Philippine people. For the month that the display was presented, more than 100,000 people attended the exhibit.[10]

Chapter VIII: Fiftieth Anniversary Celebration

By the beginning of 1945 the war in Europe was drawing to a close and there was hope that the struggle with Japan in the Pacific would also soon come to an end. With guarded optimism that in the very near future peace was a real expectation for the nation and the world, The New York Botanical Garden began to turn its attention to other matters——those affairs more closely and more directly associated with the institution. The year 1945 marked the fiftieth anniversary of the founding of The New York Botanical Garden; and there was a great desire that the event would be marked with the attention and the ceremony that the occasion deserved. In addition, The Garden's various administrators realized that there was a great need for modernization of the buildings, grounds and facilities; and this necessitated the need for a campaign to raise a large sum of money. This fund raising campaign was essential for The New York Botanical Garden to maintain its place of excellence as one of the world's leading centers for botanical research, knowledge, teaching, and beauty. As one of the pre—eminent botanical institutions in the world, The Garden by 1945 prided itself in all aspects of plant life and realized that through many different enterprises it had influenced millions of people throughout this planet. In fifty years The Garden's work and influence had gone beyond the New York area and beyond the borders of the United States; the institution's impact was international. In order to modernize the institution the decision was wisely made that for the fiftieth anniversary the institution's international dimension and the fund raising campaign would all be linked together. The institution had reached a milestone, certainly the most significant up to that stage of its development. The Garden, therefore, decided to use the occasion to position itself for even greater growth, more momentous contributions and a more profound international impact in the coming decades.

The New York Botanical Garden began with a self—study of the institution's origin, nature, purpose, development, contributions, achievements and future plans. This self—study, contained in a brochure entitled "Fiftieth Anniversary FACTS About The New York Botanical Garden", was then brought to the attention of individuals and institutions in the public and private sector.[1]

"FACTS" pointed out that the Institution came into existence in 1895 through the concerted efforts of far—sighted individuals, including a number of very influential citizens of New York, and with the institutional support of Columbia University and the Torrey Botanical Club. Fifty years later The New York Botanical Garden embodied 230 acres of prime real estate (with an assessed evaluation of $15,935,000), containing very scenic property, attractive buildings and valuable equipment, in the Bronx Park area of New York City.[2]

The importance of The Garden, actually any botanical garden, rested mainly in the fact that it dealt with the vital significance of plant life to the human race. Plants form the basis of all other living forms, including oxygen, food, coal, wood, oil, shelter and clothing. In industry, plant products provided employment for millions of individuals and produced revenues in the billions of dollars. This included such industries as the production of turpentine, resin, lacquer, paper, cordage, cheese and fermented liquids. The study of plant life helped to provide a greater understanding of heredity, genetics, enzymes, cell division and viral diseases. Such diseases as tuberculosis, pneumonia, cholera, dysentery, typhoid fever and fungous ailment stemmed from plant life and constituted in 1945 a third of all human maladies. Plant life at that time also constituted one of the main therapeutic agents for diseases——that is, plants provided such remedies as penicillin, quinine, digitalis and morphine. Lastly, The Garden was a great source of "beauty, inspiration, restfulness and recreation".[3]

Since the beginning of World War II The Garden had contributed very meaningfully to the war effort. It provided trained personnel for the production of quinine, insecticides, drugs, fibers, rubber and for service in tropical regions. The institution furnished seeds, plant material, educational films for the armed services and data on useful and poisonous plants. For the general public, The Garden introduced and developed numerous and varied programs to encourage the development of Victory Gardens.[4]

When looking for the assets and achievements of The New York Botanical Garden over the past fifty years, the self—study discovered some startling accomplishments. The institution possessed an immense collection of more than 12,000 living plants representing an assortment that was truly international. There was a herbarium of more than 2,200,000 specimens with a complementary library of 51,000 volumes of monographs and 200,000 pamphlets and journals dealing with horticulture and botany. The Garden had an excellent record of publications produced by an eminent scientific staff and highly qualified associates——the publications amounted to the equivalent of 400 volumes of 300 pages each. It had developed over the years a fine botanical museum, the only one of its kind in the United States, with a distinguished horticultural staff that had already achieved an international reputation.

The Garden's achievements in the fields of horticulture and botany produced truly outstanding contributions both to the scientific community and to the human family. The institution had been credited with naming and describing 5,500 of the 350,000 plants known in 1945. There were contributions to the field of plant reproduction and physiology, including at that time research into disease—suppressing substances produced by molds that yielded results analogous to the effects of penicillin. The Garden had conducted studies of certain plants that proved to be important for industry and the medical profession——specifically Cinchona (quinine), Strychnos (strychnine), Erythrina (alkaloids) and curare, the latter at that time had proved effective in treating certain types of heart disease. Guide manuals on the flora of most of the United States as well as similar texts on Canada, Bermuda, the Virgin Islands, the Bahamas, Puerto Rico and the Hawaiian Islands had been published in addition to such important scientific periodicals as "Mycologia, Brittonia and North American Flora". Productive research had been conducted on the culture of plants, shrubs and trees for the home and for economic applications, as well as the control of diseases associated with these plants. In general, The Garden had carried on noteworthy experiments, conducted more than one hundred and fifty expeditions that had increased the world's botanical knowledge, had maintained a fine library, herbarium, laboratories, conservatories and had developed a knowledgeable, experienced and highly respected staff; and through these highly developed facilities and personnel the public, commerce, industry and government had been excellently well—served. For the general public there had been developed lecture series and programs of varying lengths, some of them the first of their kind in the United States.[5]

A special relationship had always been maintained with Columbia University. Columbia's herbarium and botanical library had been deposited at The New York Botanical Garden. The Director of The Garden traditionally had been given the academic rank of full professor of botany at Columbia, which institution at that time was also represented on the Garden's Board of Managers by four appointees. Students at Columbia, as well as at nearby Fordham University, were entitled to take at The Garden courses for advanced degrees in botany.[6]

By 1945 the international reputation of The Garden was well known, firmly established and not without merit. On the list of the "American Men of Science" there were 102 "eminent" botanists representing forty—one educational and research establishments. The Garden was only one of five of these institutions that had five or more members. The botanical section of the National Academy of Science contained the names of twenty—three active members spread out among seventeen institutions. The Garden in 1945 was only one of two institutions that had two or more members. At the last International Botanical Congress held at Amsterdam, Holland, in 1935 (undoubtedly meetings of the Congress were interrupted by the events surrounding World War II) there were one hundred and sixty—eight institutions with representation.

The New York Botanical Garden was one of only seven 5—vote institutions——on a par internationally with The Royal Botanic Gardens at Kew, England; the British Museum; the Museum d'Histoire

Naturelle of Paris; Berlin's Botanisher Garten und Museum; and Geneva's Jardin Botanique.[7]

In the foreseeable future The Garden fully expected to be in the forefront of research into plant life and its benefits to the human race. Undoubtedly World War II spurred new developments, but also made for the realization that there still remained much to be learned. Scientifically the institution's staff realized that only their imagination, ingenuity and skills would limit their research accomplishments in the area of plant life. Medically, penicillium notatum, the source of penicillin, was only one of thousands of molds that contained material with life—saving qualities, perhaps more potent than penicillin itself. There were still at that time 150,000 plants still unknown to the scientific community. Quite conceivably many of these were as vitally important to medicine as was the discovery of the uses of cinchona (quinine), the foxglove (digitalis) or the poppy (morphine). Economically, fewer than one thousand of the 350,000 known plants in the world were used by the human race. In addition, there were in 1945 about 150,000 plants that remained to be discovered and analyzed, with the resulting knowledge disseminated. The remaining "unknowns" in this area of research were too enormous to calculate. Finally, during World War II The Garden had participated in the program of stimulating millions to grow Victory Gardens. With the end of the war many maintained an interest in gardening, perhaps in the area of ornamental plants as "a source of inspiration, spiritual comfort and physical and mental relaxation". The New York Botanical Garden, therefore, decided to remain in the forefront of providing encouragement and information for those inclined toward developing their horticultural interests as a "break" from the cares of everyday life.[8]

The New York Botanical Garden, with its unique location in the great metropolitan area of New York, was in a position to impact internationally upon the fields of botany and horticulture. Garden administrators pictured the institution developing into a great, international "botanical university", where the facilities were made globally available "for scientific research, educational work and horticultural display". The extent of this impact depended upon a great fund—raising campaign.

At that time the cost of maintaining the institution was almost entirely met by the City of New York. Scientific and educational projects, however, were supported mainly by gifts, membership fees and interest from the endowment. On June 30, 1944, the book value of the endowment fund was $2,610,422 and the market value was $2,916,968. Since 1930, however, income had declined precipitously by about $75,000 a year. This was a result of a decrease in interest rates and a decline in gift giving. As a result, talented, key personnel were sacrificed and valuable programs reduced for the sake of economy. Not only must these assets and programs be restored, but the institution's level of expertise had to be elevated.

As part of "FACT", the self—study of The Garden, the Board of Managers scrutinized, over a period of a year, the existing state, needs and requirements of the institution. It then set goals for meeting the level of excellence expected of an eminent, international botanical garden. This self—study disclosed that financially a minimum need was $6,580,000, dispersed over $2,305,000 for capital disbursement and $4,275,000 for additional endowment funds. The post—war expenditures conceived as necessary by the Board included $300,000 for participation in the planned goals of the City of New York and $1,680,000 provided by the City for improvements in the grounds and the physical facilities. In addition, the sum of $1,250,000 was needed in mid—twentieth century for the following:

1) A Curator of South American Tropical Botany. This was a little known area of exploration and study that was destined shortly to be of major significance in the industrial, commercial and medical sectors.

2) A Curator of Economic Botany. The significance of this field was not going to be ignored, especially in the light of the discoveries made during World War II. The present uses and the potential for the future of known and unknown plant life demanded that special attention be given to this area.

3) A Laboratory for the Physiology of Fungi. Again the recent war brought to light the importance of investigating tropical fungus diseases. In addition, the myriad and vital uses of fungi and molds in medicine and industry had developed into an entirely new and exciting field of study.

4) Popularizing *The Journal* of The Garden. The Board of Managers envisioned and desired that the *Journal* was destined to become the National Geographic of botany and horticulture.

5) Museum Endowment. The creation of more varied and exciting programs was necessary to serve, instruct and delight the public, a major goal of any botanical garden.

6) Special, Outdoor Garden Displays. In this area The Board of Managers desired to make the post—war Garden "the outstanding beauty spot of its kind in the world".[9] For these projects The Garden itself had to raise $4,900,000 by private subscription.

The week of May 13, to May 20, 1945, was set aside to mark the fiftieth anniversary of The New York Botanical Garden. During the week's celebrations the nature, purposes, accomplishments, the post—war plans, the fund—raising campaign and the international dimension of The Garden were all stressed and brought to the attention of the public and the government.

On Sunday, May 13, an elaborate ceremony was held on the lawn stretching down from the museum building, with a speakers' rostrum erected on the lower portion near the main entrance to The Garden. To mark the occasion Fiorello La Guardia, the famous Mayor of New York City, unveiled a plaque rededicating the New York Botanical Garden to a second half century of service to the citizens of New York and the people of the world at large for the preservation, dissemination and advancement of knowledge about plants and for the education and recreation of the public.

A number of the dignitaries, both from the private and public sector, re-marked of the importance of The Garden and the occasion that prompted the attendance of such a large gathering of people. Mayor La Guardia spoke of the most important task of The Garden as that of research and education. He promised that his administration, and hoped that future administrations, would foster the goals of the institution, and prevent politics from interfering in the relationship. After acclaiming and congratulating the institution for fifty year of splendid ac-complishments, the Mayor remarked that botany had changed so much in the past few decades that a new study of plant life had practically emerged; thus necessi-tating the need for the most modern of facilities at The Garden. His Honor, in commending The Garden in its decision to modernize its facilities, described the efforts of his administration in establishing the Public Health Research Institute under the Department of Health. The Mayor hoped that both institutions would cooperate in the future to make great contributions to humanity.[10]

Robert Moses, the well—known and indefatigable Commissioner of Parks for the City of New York, called upon The Garden to continue to develop the natural beauties of the grounds. He urged the institution not to forget the visitors who possessed very little scientific knowledge, but came to the Park for recrea-tion. With improved public transportation and the greater use of the automobile, Commissioner Moses fully anticipated that more such persons would visit The Garden and expected to be provided with facilities for their enjoyment.

Joseph R. Swan, President of The New York Botanical Garden, stressed that the institution was determined to enlarge upon its world—wide reputation for research and for being a repository of scientific knowledge. He pointed out that The Garden did receive a substantial subsidy from New York City, but greatly relied upon the private sector for gifts. President Swan underscored the impor-tance of private support if The Garden was to achieve its potential.[11]

On Saturday, May 19, as part of the fiftieth anniversary celebration, The New York Botanical Garden rededicated its facilities, knowledge and research to the service of all the people in all the nations of the world. Called International Day the ceremony was held in the Museum Building and was attended by some two hundred and fifty people, including representatives from Canada, Poland, Great Britain, India, Chile and Yugoslavia. Dr. William J. Robbins, Director of the Garden, informed those in attendance that forty—one congratulatory messages had been received from various botanical and educational institutions throughout the world. He added that at that time there were at The Garden 12,000 varieties of foreign plants and that the institution's publications were being sent to forty—five different foreign nations, all of these undertakings, of course, enlarged the international dimension of the organization. President Swan again spoke of the institution's long—standing reputation for research and scientific knowledge, but on this occasion stressed the international character of its service to the entire human race. Because of the devastation wrought upon the peoples and lands of Europe during World War II, humanity looked even more intently upon the United States for leadership in all fields of endeavor. Swan closed with the following remarks:

> The New York Botanical Garden, with its long—standing tradition of service and achievement in the cause of mankind, must look ahead to still greater opportunities for service and achievement in the future for the benefit of our own and of all nations.[12]

The celebration of the New York Botanical Garden's fiftieth anniversary lasted for eight days, from May 13, to May 20, with each day having a special theme. Monday, May 14, was Founders' Day with several direct descendants of The Garden's founders in attendance. Mrs. Andrew Carnegie, wife of one of the principal founders, was present as one of the special guests honored at the Tea given on that day. Among the special events of the week—long celebration were Children's Day, Army and Navy Day and, of course, International Day. In addition, twice each day during the week there were guided tours of the Conservatories and the Museum Building for the public. In all, the eight—day, Fiftieth Anniversary celebration attracted 137,000 visitors to The New York Botanical Garden.[13]

Chapter IX: Post World War II Years

On April 13, 1947, Joseph Swan, President of the New York Botanical Garden, and Basil O'Connor, President of the National Foundation for Infantile Paralysis, jointly announced that a new campaign against poliomyelitis (infantile paralysis) was going to be waged in the laboratories of The Garden. The search for an antibiotic capable of destroying or inactivating viruses such as those that cause infantile paralysis was financed by a five—year grant of $225,000 from the March of Dimes.

For the past several years before 1947 researchers at The Garden had been studying substances capable of inactivating bacteria. They had been able to grow more than one thousand organisms, mainly fungi, many of which demonstrated in the laboratory some evidence of being able to destroy bacteria. Dr. Robbins, Director of The Garden (1937—1957) and also Professor of Botany at Columbia University, now proposed to test the effects of these organisms on bacterial viruses, especially that virus which caused poliomyelitis. Robbins pointed out that, since the discovery of penicillin, much had been accomplished in the struggle against bacteria, but very little research in the battle against viruses. Professor Robbins' studies were aimed at determining whether there were antibiotics capable of destroying, restricting or arresting the growth of viruses. Robbins believed that probably the best strategy against poliomyelitis was to find a suitable, but weak, strain of the virus that would bring about immunization; but he did not rule out the possibility of discovering an antibiotic which would have a similar effect on other viruses. One very important advantage in The Garden's use of bacterial viruses in its experiments was speed or acceleration. "Dr. Robbins said that 100 or more substances could be investigated for antibiotic activity against bacteriophage in the time required to determine the action of one such substance in an animal virus".[1]

On Wednesday, May 10, 1950, at the opening of The New York Botanical Garden's annual five day spring festival, announcements were made concerning a number of exciting and promising discoveries made by the scientific staff of the institution. After four years of experimentation with plant molds Director Robbins disclosed to the members of the corporation's Board of Managers that a new

antibiotic compound, Illudin—M, inhibited the development of the human tuberculosis bacilli in test—tube experimentation. E. R Squibb & Sons was at that
time in the process of testing the new substance for possible toxicity on animals or
for any other impact on animal life. The Director went on to relate that Dr. Frederick Kavanagh, Dr. Annette Hervey, Dr. Marjorie Anchel and their associates
have continued to test for the veracity of Illudin—M's therapeutic value in
treating human tuberculosis. As a result of extensive experimentation Robbins
also reported that garden researchers had been able to isolate nine other antibac-
terial substances from plant molds, one of which very interestingly prevented
bacterial viruses from destroying bacteria.

Another series of experiments involved the relationship between certain very
small plants and anti—anemia vitamin B—12. The plant in question was the
one—celled alga, Euglena gracilis, which deposited the ugly greenish coat that
many people have noticed on certain ponds during the heat of summer. This plant,
it was explained, was minute (2,500 barely cover the head of a pin), and needed an
intake of vitamin B—12 to survive. Garden researchers were attempting the
following: ascertain the origin of B—12; whether other living things besides
Euglena and man needed the vitamin and finally how it produced red blood
corpuscles in humans. Garden scientists had set out, therefore, to determine the
source, nature and exact function of this indispensable vitamin in the manufacture
of human red blood corpuscles.[2]

Another program of experiments conducted by The Garden was concerned
with an inquiry into the essential factors connected with abnormal growth, with
special emphasis upon the increasing problem of cancer. Dr. R. S. de Ropp, a
member of The Garden staff, with the support of grants from the American
Cancer Society, was engaged in the study of plant tumors which in many respects
did resemble cancerous growths in animals. Dr. Robbins was not able, of course,
to predict where such experiments were going to lead The Garden staff.[3]

Lastly, Dr. Robbins addressed the issue of plant life, the world's food resources and the survival of the human family. He asserted that by employing to
the fullest extent the earth's plant resources "in the interest of our collective
self—preservation, if for nothing else", botanists were capable of, at least, post-
poning the dire emergency of terrible food shortages that have been predicted by
many experts. Charles B. Harding, President of the New York Botanical Garden,
repeated the Director's message by asserting that the institution's staff was
making great strides in finding new sources of food for all of the peoples of the
world. The President also revealed that Garden explorers were scouring the globe
to discover, collect and identify plant species that yielded significant quantities of
cortisone and other steroids needed in the medical profession for the treatment of
various illnesses and for the maintenance of healthy humans.[4]

On May 10, 1950, Dr. H. A Gleason, Head Curator of the New York Botanical Garden, informed the Board of Managers the very important and interesting story of how, historically, the institution become vitally interested and

active in exploring South America, especially the northern portion of that Continent. Throughout the nineteenth century American exploration concentrated upon North America, while the tropical region south of the American border was hardly visited. A great deal needed to be learned about the botany and horticulture of North America; and this was enough to keep American explorers and scientists busily confined to our continent. In 1885, however, Dr. Henry H. Rusby, later Curator of The Garden's economic collections, conducted one of the earliest, American—led trips to South America, an expedition into the mountainous regions of Bolivia. Upon his return Rusby gave to Dr. N. L. Britton, then Professor of Botany at Columbia University, botanical specimens from Bolivia of which Britton had no personal knowledge, nor, about which, was he able to find much information. Almost all the knowledge about the botany of South America had been discovered by Europeans and there were few books in the United States about their discoveries. Britton's natural curiosity, however, had been stimulated and this prompted the famous trip of Nathaniel and Elizabeth Britton to the Royal Botanic Gardens at Kew in Great Britain that, as already related, led ultimately to the formation of the New York Botanical Garden.

After the establishment of The Garden, Britton selected the thorough search and study of North America, including Mexico, Central America and the West Indies, as the area of concentration for the new institution. His own personal area of concentration was the West Indies, to which he devoted himself with some thirty years of exploration, research, study and publication. More than forty expeditions by Britton or one of his associates from The Garden covered the area from Jamaica and Cuba through Puerto Rico and Haiti and the smaller islands as far as Trinidad.

> Year by year our collections grew, until he had built up the largest, the finest, the most comprehensive collection of West Indian plants in the world, and Britton, our director, and Wilson, his right—hand man, had become international authorities on the plant life of all the islands.[5]

Dr. Gleason explained that Britton's expertise, however, presented accompanying problems. These plants of the West Indies frequently were closely related to those of South America; often it proved troublesome to differentiate plants from the West Indies from similar ones growing, for example, in Venezuela. It became indispensable, therefore, to add northern South America to The Garden's field of operation. This decision then posed the problem of covering a vast territory: a great expanse of land, thousands of miles from the mouth of the Amazon River to the Pacific and at least a thousand miles from north to south. The expanse covered thousands of square miles, unmapped, with lofty mountains never observed by white men and great, unexplored rivers. Britton in 1917 wisely decided that this very necessary undertaking in South America was too great for one institution and must be a cooperative effort; the National Herbarium in Washington, D.C. and the Gray Herbarium of Harvard University were approached and agreed to participate in the project. Later the Chicago Museum of Natural History, the Philadelphia Academy of Sciences and the University of California aided in the venture. The New York Botanical Garden, however, had always been the most prominent institution in the South American undertaking.

When Dr. Gleason joined The Garden staff in 1919 he was designated to organize and lead this project in the northern reaches of the Continent of South America. For the next twenty years this research project, a rather herculean affair, became the center of his professional life. It was generally assumed that the Europeans had accumulated a considerable amount of scientific knowledge in this area of the world, but that assumption proved to be unfounded. There were still tens of thousands of square miles where the knowledge of plant life was unknown. No botanist had ever been to this vast area of the northern portion of the continent of South America.

Since 1917 there had been numerous expeditions into this wild, unknown region of the world that constituted the northern segment of South America. It was the segment of the world that Arthur Conan Doyle used as a place setting for his story, "The Lost World". This gave Gleason's listeners an idea of the inaccessibility and vastness of the area. Into this vast, mostly unknown region, bands of explorers and scientists penetrated over the years: Broadway into French Guiana; Maguire and Samuelsson into Surinam; Hitchcock, Smith, Maguire and Pinkus into British Guiana; Rusby, Johnson, Pittier and Maguire into Venezuela; Pennell, Killip, Hazen, Smith and Rusby into Colombia; Hitchcock and Camp into Ecuador; Smith and Killip into the upper Amazon. And these were the ones officially connected with the New York Botanical Garden; there were others from the other institutions, but everyone profited by the joint venture because all knowledge was shared. The advent of World War II spurred greater interest in this region. There was created a great need for new sources of rubber and quinine; many American botanists ranged over a vast area from the mouth of the Amazon to the high Andes Mountains searching for new sources of these vital materials, returning with thousands of specimens of many different types of plants

By 1950 Dr. Gleason gave this evaluation of the plant collections at the New York Botanical Garden: of the plants from French Guiana, second only to those in Paris; of the plants of Dutch Surinam, second only to those at Utrecht in Holland; of Venezuela and Colombia, second only to those in the National Herbarium in Washington, D.C.; of Bolivia, Ecuador, British Guiana, and those of the very remote mountainous region of southern Venezuela, probably second to none. The Garden had a splendid collection from Brazil's Amazon region, but the Curator was not able to rank it comparatively. In general, Gleason stated in his report that, concerning the northern part of South America, "The collections here at home are far better than those of Europe"[6]

At the corporation's annual meeting on May 15, 1952, Charles B. Harding, President of The New York Botanical Garden, announced the plans for the renovation of the old Bronx River mill into a restaurant. When the Lorillard Family relocated their snuff manufacturing operation in 1790 from Manhattan to the Bronx River Gorge area, part of the purchase included an old wooden snuff mill. In 1840 the Lorillards replaced this old structure with the present stone building, in which eventually much of the nation's snuff was processed. Since the departure of the Lorillards in 1870 the building had for the most part remained unused and lately had been utilized for the storage of tools. For more than half of its one hundred and twelve year history, therefore, the building was hardly used.

Built immediately south of the spectacular Bronx River Falls and the Great Gorge, it was located in an Adirondack Mountain/Forest Primeval—like setting. The old building was constructed on sloping land bordering the Bronx River and was erected three floors high on the land side and four stories on the river side. The plans for the new restaurant were drawn up by the architectural firm of Brown, Lawford and Forbes. The cost of renovation came to $166,000. The refurbishing of the old mill was financed by an appropriation from The Garden and through the generosity of the P. Lorillard Tobacco Company, the Parks Department of the City of New York and especially Mrs. Harold I. Pratt, with the latter contributing $88,000. The plans called for the river—level floor to be converted into a restaurant with bay windows and an outdoor dining terrace stretching toward the Bronx River. The first or ground level floor was designated as a meeting and conference hall, check room and comfort station, with the third floor used for storage.[7]

As much as possible the building was left in its original form and condition in recognition of its historical and architectural importance. Century—old wooden beams on the floor of the conference room were not removed but left exposed and untouched, displaying where the machinery for the old grinding stones had been affixed. During the restoration work three millstones were unearthed fifteen feet below the base of the west wall. One stone was native New England granite, forty—seven and one half inches in diameter, thirteen inches thick with a ten by seven inch hole. The other two appeared to be volcanic, surrounded by wrought iron with two wrought iron loops attached for the block and tackle. These last two millstones were the same diameter as the granite stone, but seven inches thick with a hole nine and one—half by twelve inches.

The Garden authorities were very interested to learn about the two volcanic stones and their journey to the grounds. It turned out that the likely origin and story how of these stones got to the famous mill were very fascinating. To find the answers Dr. Brian Mason, chief mineralogist and curator of geology at New York's American Museum of Natural History, was called—in to analyze the composition of the two volcanic stones. The curator reported that they were porous basalt, containing essentially the minerals augite and feldspar. This type of rock was common in many parts of the world, but not in Eastern United States and Canada. Concluding that they were not dragged over the Rocky Mountains from California in the period of the mid—nineteenth century, the American Museum expert judged that the volcanic rocks were excavated in southwestern Germany or southern Italy where similar stone was commonplace at that time. Dr. Mason assumed that the Lorillard Family had the volcanic millstones fashioned in a European quarry, carried by clipper ship to the docks on Manhattan Island in New York City and then hauled by bullock carts to their snuff mill on the Bronx River. During the restoration work one of the millstones was embedded in the paving in front of the main entrance to the mill. In 1954 the renovation was completed and the Snuff Mill Restaurant was opened to the public.[8]

On May 19, 1952, President Charles B. Harding announced that The Garden would soon begin the construction of a $1,000,000 laboratory building. The cost of the building was estimated at about $800,000, with an additional $200,000 needed for modern equipment and other auxiliary expenses. At the time of the announcement Harding also mentioned that about $500,000 had already been pledged by private individuals and that the City of New York had set aside an additional $150,000 for construction of the new building. Construction of the laboratory was scheduled to begin when The Garden had raised the entire $1,000,000, which sum was expected to be on hand by the end of 1952. Meanwhile The Garden contacted the architectural firm of Brown, Lawford and Forbes, which soon presented preliminary sketches for the planned building.

The Garden's Director, Dr. William J. Robbins, outlined the great need that the institution had for a new, modern laboratory. In 1952 scientific investigation and experimentation were conducted in the cramped basement quarters of the museum building, a very handsome structure but fifty years old and entirely inadequate for the research needs of The Garden. The Garden's collection of plants and herbaria had reached 2,500,000, which constituted one of the largest in the world. At that time the staff was intently engaged in important research on vitamin B—12, viral diseases, infantile paralysis and cancer. Added space was also essential to accommodate the large number of advanced students who wished to work with the staff on the various projects then being conducted. The training and development of young and talented people into specialists in the field of botany was of the utmost importance to The Garden. Dr. Robbins was not only The Director of the Institution, but also Professor of Botany at Columbia University where many highly regarded students sought him as their teacher and mentor. Thus the new laboratory was designed to become a center for the study of the physiology and biochemistry of plant life and serve as a magnate to train new botanists. President Harding commented: "This is the most important thing that has happened to the garden in many years. Never in our history has there been so great a need for this type of biological work"[9] In 1956 the new research facility was dedicated and is now known as the Charles B. Harding Laboratory, to honor the man who was very instrumental in the creation, financing and construction of the new laboratory building.

Dr. William J. Robbins in his "Annual Report for 1953" reiterated that the two main objectives of The Garden were to provide a place of beauty and recreation for the general public and to make its library, herbarium, plant collections, laboratories and staff available for research for the betterment of the human race. The institution was dedicated to continue to provide these services in spite of increasing financial difficulties; and starting in the early 1950s the financial problems for The Garden became a continuing burden for the administration. In his report for the year 1953, given at the annual meeting on May 20, 1954, Robbins outlined the substantial progress and additions that had been made throughout the past year as follows:

> Additions were made to the Montgomery Conifer Collection, the interior of the major part of the Conservatory was reconstructed, substantial progress was made on the reconstruction of the Lorillard Snuff Mill, reconstruction of a section of the interior driveway was begun, plans to revamp the Rose Garden were made and construction initiated, plans for the construction of a laboratory were begun; an expedition to Venezuela was successfully completed; progress on the preparation of a flora of California and one of the northwestern United States was made, the publication of *The New Britton and Brown Illustrated Flora of the Northeastern United States and Adjacent Canada* was completed; flower shows in the Conservatory were re—established; significant additions were made to the library and to the herbarium; exhibits were staged in the Museum Building, and many other special events were held.

These vast and myriad achievements strained The Garden's resources and required the utmost commitment of the entire staff. These activities cost money; and institutions, like the New York Botanical Garden, that depend so heavily upon endowments, gifts and donations have been severely affected by the rising toll of inflation. Costs had thus risen but income had not been able to keep pace, largely traced to the continuing decrease in the value of the dollar. In spite of every effort to maintain a balanced budget, the financial year ending on July I, 1953, presented a deficit of $40,000. Robbins concluded his remarks on finances with the following statement: "It is hoped that means may be found to permit the budget to be balanced without sacrificing the important work of the Garden"[10] The Garden's budget, with the distinct possibility of a deficit, was the continuing, serious concern for the institution's administration in the years to come.

On May 17, 1956, Dr. William J. Robbins presented the "Report of the Director" at the Annual Meeting of the Board. This "Report", Robbins' last as The Director, became an important document because it presented an overview of the eighteen years in which he directed the institution. In his remarks Robbins outlined the many "notable improvements" made since 1938, some of which are as follows:

1) A Downtown Office was established.

2) The grounds were developed 25%, including the Montgomery Conifer Collection, the azalea planting, the Havemeyer lilacs, the Dexter rhododendrons and the property along the Bronx River Parkway.

3) The space in the Main Conservatory devoted to flowers was increased threefold.

4) The care of five additional buildings was added to maintenance, namely the Snuff Mill, Storage Building, Service Building, Compost Shed and Laboratory.

5) Public service functions were greatly increased, necessitating a considerable increase of staff in that area.

6) Retirement benefits were substantially increased.

7) The Library increased 30% from 45,916 volumes to 61,660, necessitating a consequent increase in the attention needed to service that area.

8) The herbarium increased 30% from 1,887,709 specimens to 2,460,852, with increased usage and thus added concern and care by the staff.

9) A program of laboratory research was added to the services provided by the institution.

10) Twenty—four expeditions were conducted in the United States and abroad.

11) Finally, there were many publications, books and journals, issued by The Garden.

Services for the public and the scientific community, therefore, increased; thus the Institution more than accomplished "the objectives set forth in the Act of Incorporation". The Garden, however, needed to be aware of The Director's growing apprehension over the budget. Since 1938 income had certainly increased, but had hardly kept pace with the decrease in the buying power of the dollar that was the result of inflation. He remarked that the slogan of one well—known business firm was "Progress is out most important product". Robbins believed that this slogan accurately described The Garden's activities over the past eighteen years and certainly must be maintained in the years to come. Specifically, Dr. Robbins urged that The New York Botanical Garden should include among its future plans the following: an increase in the endowment, a modern building to accommodate the Library and Herbarium and an area outside of New York City where collected plants could be grown and research conducted.[11]

Chapter X: Growth and Environmental Issues

On December 12, 1957, Charles B. Harding, President of The Garden, announced the resignation of Director William J. Robbins, the retirement to take effect on December 31, 1957. At the same time Harding announced that Dr. William C. Steere[1], Dean of the Graduate Division of Stanford University in California, was selected to succeed Robbins as the Director of The New York Botanical Garden. Since Steere planned on taking office about July, 1958, Dr. David D. Keck, Assistant Director and Head Curator, served as the interim Director.[2]

In 1958 The New York Botanical Garden started a long—desired and greatly needed Native Plant Garden. The idea for this project, however, can be traced back to the early years of the twentieth century when Mrs. Elizabeth G. Britton in 1902 became one of the prime movers in organizing the Wild Flower Preservation Society of America (succeeded in 1933 by The Wild Flower Preservation Society). In the point—of—view of Mrs. Britton and like—minded individuals there was a vital need to preserve native flora, a fact that must be brought to the attention of the general public. Through lectures, learned articles, letters and, most importantly, her personal determination the wife of the Founder of The Garden directed this campaign of conservation. Between 1912 and 1929 Mrs. Britton published in *The Journal of The New York Botanical Garden* fourteen articles on "Wild Plants Needing Protection". Finally, long after the death of Mrs. Britton, with bulldozers clearing many areas of the northeast for the construction of housing projects, shopping centers and highways the decision was made by The Garden in 1958 to create a Native Plant Garden. At this time Renee DuPont Donaldson, Mrs. Percy Douglas and the members of the Native Plant Garden Committee took up the challenge set forth many years ago by the wisdom and foresight of such pioneers of conservation as Elizabeth G. Britton and offered to create and support the much—needed, special habitat required to sustain the magnificent, increasingly rare and endangered plants of the Northeastern part of the United States. T. H. Everett, a member of The Garden, in 1964 succinctly expressed the purpose of this garden in the following terms. We will not limit our plants to those that are natural only to The Garden area. We will develop a garden "in which will be cultivated as large and representative a collection as possible of those plants that occur spontaneously in eastern North America." In regard to the design of this garden Everett remarked: "...it will be naturalistic. We expect to develop that finest type of garden, the one in which the true artist so successfully conceals his art that the effect is that of complete naturalness."

The Native Plant Garden was created as a three acre habitat of plants native to within one hundred miles of New York City. It is about three acres in size and divided into four parts:

1) A woodland section with flowering plants native to such an area;

2) The Joseph deforest Junking Limestone Garden, designed for plants that like alkaline soil;

3) The New Jersey Pine Barrens for plants that require sandy soil;

4) A carefully maintained meadowland area for plants that need a sunny, damp habitat.

The Native Plant Garden is very appropriately dedicated to the memory of Elizabeth Gertrude Knight Britton, whose great interest in horticulture and conservation inspired the creation of this particular region of the grounds. There was and remains a great need to fight for those plants on the verge of extinction and bring back those that have completely disappeared from the New York City area. Quite accurately the Native Plant Garden was the visual expression of Nancy Newhall's philosophy in her book, *This is the American Earth*, that conservation is defined as "humanity fighting for the future".[3]

By the early 1960s the herbarium collection had reached the staggering total of over three million specimens. The library, which in part serviced the herbarium in a complementary fashion, had grown to over 70,000 volumes and more than 300,000 unbound publications. Both the herbarium and the library were housed in the Museum Building. It was obvious, however, that the library had grown to such an extent that a new wing had to be added to the Museum building, both to house the vast collection and to serve the researchers who used the facility. In 1961 construction was begun on a six story addition that was designed to house the Library and the Administrative offices. In 1965 the Harriet Barnes Pratt Library Wing[4] was opened and was dedicated to a long—time, invaluable contributor and associate of The Garden. In 1972 the Administrative, Educational and Publication offices were moved to a new addition to the Museum Building named the Watson Science and Education Building.[5]

May 1, 1967, was a special occasion for the New York Botanical Garden. Adorned with beautiful flowers, sparkling water falls and rare tropical foliage, The Garden welcomed two hundred guests from the scientific community, the business world, the government sector and cultural affairs. That evening there was a gala, formal dinner to mark three noteworthy Garden events. The participants celebrated: the institution's completion of seventy—five years of outstanding service to humanity; the announcement of a $40 million development campaign to expand over the next twenty—five years the grounds, facilities and capabilities of the organization; and the designation of The New York Botanical Garden as a Registered National Historic Landmark.

The Honorable George B. Hartzog, Jr., Director of the National Park Service, presented to the Botanical Garden an attractive document with his signature and that of Stewart L. Udall, Secretary of the United States Department of the Interior. Also presented was a bronze plaque that was positioned on one of the two Corinthian columns at the main entrance to the Museum Building. It was installed next to a considerably older plaque commemorating the founding of The Garden. The National Historic Landmark plaque very aptly read:

> The New York Botanical Garden has been designated a Registered National Historic Landmark under the provisions of the Historic Sites Act of August 21, 1935. This site possesses exceptional value in commemorating or illustrating the history of the United States. U.S. Department of the Interior, National Park Service, 1967.[6]

During the presentation ceremony Mr. Hartzog stated that the United States Congress had given to the National Park Service the assignment of recognizing sites that had greatly contributed to the historical development of the Unites States. This task is accomplished through the Registry of National Historic Landmarks, a designation that meant certain, carefully—selected sites have great national significance as a result of their cultural, historical, educational and scientific contributions to America and the American people. The New York Botanical Garden was singled out for this distinction because for over seventy years the institution had striven to discover everything there is to know about plant life and then to communicate this knowledge not only to the scientific community but to all humanity. The accomplishments of The Garden have gained for the organization an international reputation as one of the world's outstanding botanical gardens. Then The Director of the National Park Service paid a very noble compliment to The Garden when he explained to those in attendance that "The legacy of The New York Botanical Garden is knowledge, and its ideal is truth and service. We do not want these values to be neglected; indeed, we should like today to commend them to the Nation"[7]

Director Hartzog familiarized the audience with the United States Government's long—existing concern, an anxiety that went back more than one hundred years. This apprehension was related to the growth of American civilization across the vast western wilderness and the basic freedom of the American people to fulfill their individual needs. These two elements began to conflict and this conflict, as the government recognized, was only going to get worse. Thus, more than a century ago the American government began to involve itself with the conservation of the nation's vast, marvelous wonders of nature and the preservation of our historical treasures. From this desire there emerged, in 1872, the establishment of Yellowstone National Park. Evolving from this event there developed the National Park System that by 1967 numbered two hundred and forty parks visited by more than 150,000,000 people each year.[8]

Developing from a similar concern for the preservation of the planet's natural wonders came, in the words of Mr. Hartzog, the inspiration and desire of Professor and Mrs. Nathaniel Lord Britton to establish The New York Botanical Garden. In the years following the establishment of this institution the goals of The Garden have been analogous to those of the National Park Service: research, education and service to the general public. Since its inception The Botanical Garden has achieved its expressed commitment to the "instruction of the people". Undeniably the institution has contributed enormously to the public's delight and appreciation of the environment. In the Garden's campaign to establish a new ethic among Americans, an ethic of world—wide concern for the environment and the science of botany, Hartzog stated unequivocally that the credentials of The New York Botanical Garden are remarkably outstanding: the largest herbarium and the finest botanical library in the Western Hemisphere; discoveries such as the process of 'puffing' rice, seedless grapes and antibiotics; and a publication program in the field of botany unsurpassed throughout the world. Director George B. Hartzog concluded his observations with the following complimentary remarks:

> It is, therefore, a rare pleasure to designate The New York Botanical Garden as a Registered National Historic Landmark for its significant contribution to human knowledge and welfare through its programs of research, publishing and education.[9]

In the 1950s and the 1960s the concerns of The New York Botanical Garden and like—minded institutions and individuals turned toward the environmental problems that began to face the world in an ever increasing and threatening manner. It was no mere coincidence that at this time The Garden created a Native Plant Garden to save plants of the northeast, many of which were threatened by extinction. The construction of a new, modern library wing was also a demonstration of the institution's desire to house, save, safeguard and make readily available the accumulated botanical knowledge in its possession. The designation of The Garden as a National Historic Landmark was the American government's recognition of the corporation's long—time interest in safeguarding the environment and the expression of confidence of further research in the area of ecology. The New York Botanical Garden had always considered protecting the world's resources by increasing humanity's knowledge of the plant kingdom to be a sacred trust, a main purpose of the institution.

The preservation of the planet's living organisms now had become an effort of great urgency because of the increasing exploitation of our resources for the sake of immediate profit. Conservation and preservation was the theme of a special lead essay by Dr. William C. Steere, Director of The New York Botanical

Garden, in a 1967 issue of *The Garden Journal*. The "ruthless exploitation of anything that will yield a profit now, without regard to its unfortunate effects on future generations," Steere likened to the advertisements that encouraged people: "'Travel now, pay later'". Such an attitude toward the planet's resources was unacceptable, especially since the unfortunate consequences for future generations are certain and the extent of the disaster totally incalculable.[10]

Dr. Steere pointed out that many species of plants are extinct because of changes in the environment or the actions of man. Others are heading toward extinction. A fact that cannot be ignored is that "A species of animal or plant, once extinct, is gone forever—it can never be recreated, since it represents the end product of tens or hundreds of millions of years of evolution". He went on to remind his readers that "Man has hastened the disappearance of organisms already teetering on the brink of extinction, as the dodo bird; on the other hand, to his eternal credit, he has also rescued other species from oblivion". The destructive actions of the human race speak for themselves, but the efforts made to conserve species marked for eventual extinction present interesting possibilities, according to Steere.

In Japan, Ginkgo biloba, commonly known as the maidenhair tree, was saved from extinction by temple priests. Over the decades the monks had noticed its increasing scarcity in the wild and realized it was heading for extinction. The priests took the extraordinary step of planting the ginkgo tree on temple grounds where it has flourished to the present day and is held in great esteem by the Japanese people. The tree is also planted widely on American city streets because it is remarkably resistant to smoke and soot. According to Steere, ginkgo biloba "is not known today at all in the wild, yet the fossil record shows that many millions of years ago it was spread widely through the Northern Hemisphere, including Europe and North America".

Another interesting tale is the story of Metasequoia glyptostroboides, the dawn redwood, which is a relative of Sequoiadendron giganteum, the famous giant redwoods of the Sierra Nevada mountain range of California. The dawn redwood was thought to be a fossil plant before 1945, when it was discovered living in one of the remotest sections of southwest China. Some dawn redwoods were brought to The New York Botanical Garden where they thrived. In fact, they were found to be hardier than their more famous relatives, the giant redwoods. As a result of the interest and efforts of The Garden, seeds were distributed and by 1967 the dawn redwood was widely planted throughout the eastern portion of the United States.

Dr. Steere presented his conclusions in very clear terms, terms that can be easily understood and used in the twenty—first century. In the final analysis, the simple, but vitally important, lesson learned from the efforts of the Japanese temple and The New York Botanical Garden is that something can and must be done when a species is threatened with extinction, whether as a result of environmental changes or the indiscriminate, injurious actions of man. It must be recognized, however, that, no matter how ecologically minded humanity may become, certain species are heading for extinction, either because of natural changes in the environment or the indiscriminate indifference of a relatively few individuals. These threatened species, however, almost certainly can remain cultivated in places such as The New York Botanical Garden, long after the wild varieties have vanished. The human race thus can and must learn to conserve and preserve all species of life, for replacing them is impossible once they are extinct.[11]

On April 25—26, The New York Botanical Garden, in conjunction with The Rockefeller University, sponsored a symposium, "Challenge for Survival 1968: Land, Air and Water for Man in Megalopolis". The theme of the symposium was the threat to life that is posed by the growth of metropolitan areas; a growth so vast that one no longer speaks of a metropolis but of a megalopolis. Demographers at that time recognized, for example, that on the Eastern seaboard urban life stretched almost continuously from the City of Boston to Washington, D.C. The Garden acknowledged this growing problem, with the accompanying threats to all forms of life, by calling for this symposium, at which various experts presented their views in learned papers.

A paper read by Dr. S. H. Hutner, Associate Research Director of the Haskins Laboratories in New York and Adjunct Professor of Fordham University, was adapted for publication in the *Garden Journal*.[12] The theme of the paper, entitled "The Urban Botanical Garden: An Academic Wildlife Preserve", was that "A botanical garden retains the links to earth needed for our urbanized society to stay vital and creative".

Hutner singled out the land—grant university of the American mid—west and far west as one of the great endowments of the United States to the academic community, and perhaps even to the history of civilization. It was designed as a "symbiosis between university and community". This type of university was founded and pledged to serve the community; that is, answering the needs and solving the problems of a specific area. The community (usually agricultural, but also mining in mountain areas) gave immediate support in the form of financial backing for the various departments and programs established by such an academic institution. In the early history of the land—grant universities there was a great deal of "ground—breaking" to be done. A tradition of non—interference was established; development and practices were left to those involved in higher education. Even when the university judged that additional and substantial funding was necessary to solve specific, serious problems, the community was there to provide the supplementary financial resources. In addition, the supplemental money was provided without attached conditions. The university was judged competent to use this financial support in the best manner, thus guaranteeing the traditional academic freedom of the university community. A great trust developed between the university and the general community, thus helping to "make 'peasant' inapropos in describing the heavily capitalized American farmers who grow most of our food". Hutner praised the American land—grant universities, "once derided as cow colleges," for largely evading "the perils of utilitarianism and babbittry on one hand, and on the other the kind of nineteenth century Oxbridgian mandarinism that T. H. Huxley so fiercely opposed".

Hutner pointed out that the New York area faced a number of serious problems. One concerned the superb Hudson River resources, now seriously threatened by increasing pollution.. The Hudson has its source in the Adirondack Mountains at the uncontaminated Lake Tear o' the Clouds, where the water is pristine clear and clean. Before reaching the town of Saratoga it begins to receive an infusion of pollutants; at this point, the pollutants are creamery wastes from the dairy farms of the area. Passing through the flat area below Saratoga the Hudson River waters becomes contaminated by waste from paper mills. The River then receives the raw sewage of such cities as Troy, Albany and Poughkeepsie, where at the latter city sea water begins to mix with the fresh water of the Adirondacks. In the harbor of New York the Hudson River encounters the discharges of the bilges of the numerous ships and the release of the waste of the metropolitan area, which Hutner refers to as a "septic tank". The pollution of the Hudson River, according to Hutner, must be checked and the process reversed, if the River is ever once again going to afford millions of people with a source of recreation, scenic beauty and a food supply.

Professor Hutner believed that the growing ecological problems of the New York metropolitan area, which was rapidly becoming part of a megalopolis, needed an infusion of new ideas and new relationships between institutions. Urban areas did not have a tradition of land grant colleges. In addition, city—based institutions of higher learning had never been deeply involved with the problems associated with the pollution of the environment and the obvious need of developing programs and departments of ecology. And this is where The New York Botanical Garden was in a position to play a vital role, according to Hutner. Such institutions need to inaugurate a relationship between botanical gardens and universities. The development of such relationships benefits society and sustains the well being of both the university and the botanical garden. For example, the growing problem of cancer, especially in urban areas, requires the close attention of botanical societies. Cancer is a malady of "multicellularity", which makes it a problem that is very difficult to analyze and solve. All options to solve this problem must be explored, including the study of plant life. From such institutions as The New York Botanical Garden may come the scientific investigators and the knowledge to solve such human disorders as cancer.

Hutner maintained that city universities need to develop themselves into the urban counterpart of the land grant college. They must become "urban grant universities" to solve urban problems, just as the land grant colleges helped and continue to assist the agricultural community in solving its problems. He concluded that establishments such as The New York Botanical Garden need to grow into a breeding ground for academics, who would then return to their universities imbued with new ideas and an enthusiasm for change and revitalization. Professor Hutner presented the intriguing concept that the aim of professional scientific societies rooted in natural history, namely such institutions as The New York Botanical Garden, "is to produce art: to depict the creatures and tell what they do. Scientific societies and institutions must be the new Medicis".[13]

Since its foundation in 1895 The New York Botanical Garden in its scientific capacity had mainly been a resource center for scientists, scholars, researchers and students. The Garden, however, had also served the needs and interests of the ordinary home gardener. Every week there were hundreds of calls and visits by home gardeners seeking information about the selection and cultivation of certain plants for this area, the needs of particular species and the prevention and treatment of plants afflicted by pests and diseases. The Garden staff invariably did its best to help each and every person who made an inquiry. The answers given to these questions, not only fulfilled the educational purpose of the founding of The Garden, but also was a response to the institution's and society's growing concern about the environment. The increasing and complex problems of gardeners usually could be traced to environmental issues. In response to this growing need The New York Botanical Garden in 1969 established The Plant Information Service, which became a division of the institution's famed library, with its extensive collection of scientific and reference material. The great library of The Garden had long served the public in providing such information as plant identification, disease and insect control, suggestions on landscaping, treatment of human contact with poisonous plants and general information on indoor plants and garden maintenance. Now, with the establishment of The Plant Information Service, facts and information were provided on a more formal basis.[14]

By 1976 The Service was dealing with more than seven thousand calls, fifteen hundred letters and three hundred and sixty visits each year. Although the department was a valuable public service, it was forced in 1976 to cease operation. In that year city and state funding for The Garden had been reduced because of a governmental, fiscal crisis. For the next two years such inquiries were handled by individuals from the library, the scientific area or the horticultural staffs. With all of their regular duties members of these departments did their best to answer questions from the public; but it was not an ideal arrangement. The Plant Information Service was reinstated in 1978, in answer to an obvious public need.

The office of The Plant Information Service, located on the second floor of the Watson Building, was now equipped with its own large, excellent microscope, reference books, seed catalogues and sources of information on diseases and insect pests that afflicted various types of plants. From 1982 until 1986 T. H. Everett, the celebrated horticulturist, assisted the staff in answering questions. His definitive *New York Botanical Garden Illustrated Encyclopedia of Horticulture* remained a standard reference work for the staff members of this public service program. In 1986 Ms. Dora Galitzki, who graduated from Cornell University as a specialist in woody plants, assumed the leadership of this department and was assisted by Miss Elizabeth Hall, the retired, long—time librarian of The Garden. Miss Hall graciously answered questions and gave of her time until her death in April of 1989, at the age of 90. The Plant Information Service has continued to perform the task of assisting the public with answers to their horticultural questions, some of which required extensive research in the main library This Department thus has served the public and The New York Botanical Garden in the growing concern over environmental issues, especially as to how they affect the general community.[15]

In 1971 The Institute of Ecosystem Studies, a division of The New York Botanical Garden, was established at the Mary Flagler Cary Arboretum located in Millbrook, New York, a community situated seventy miles north of New York City near the intersection of the Taconic State Parkway with Route 44. The area chosen for the Arboretum consisted of 2,000 acres of diverse habitats: deciduous and mixed—conifer woodlands, wetlands, floodplains, old fields, plants and trees that have been introduced into the area. Research at the Institute has centered upon northern temperate ecosystems, their disruption and the steps to be taken for their reclamation. The terrain chosen was topographically and geologically diverse, a condition that presented scientists with a range of environmental circumstances very conducive for research on ecosystem problems. The location even provided a two—mile stretch of stream that offered the singular opportunity to conduct aquatic research. The Institute then developed facilities that enabled scientists to conduct extended research on various ecological problems. College students (both graduate and undergraduate), local high school pupils and adult groups were offered various programs in botany and environmental studies. Lastly, for visitors there were developed nature trails and several types of gardens that provided enjoyment, in addition to affording a greater understanding of plant life. The Institute of Ecosystem Studies truly furnished the public, college students, scientific researchers and The New York Botanical Garden with the opportunity to study the environmental problems afflicting this area of the planet's northern temperate zone.[16]

In 1973 The New York Botanical Garden initiated a program to understand and reverse the environmental problems seriously affecting a waterway that cut through the Garden itself: the Bronx River. Called "The Bronx River Project", the study, undertaken by and under the direction of The Garden's Environmental Education Program, was designed to acquire a better understanding of the River, its various ecosystems, its history, its relationship with surrounding communities and the present condition of everything within and along its banks. In turn, a better understanding of the environment of the Bronx River improved scientist's perception of the planet's environment. It was a local project with important world—wide implications.[17]

After the last glacier covered the Bronx thousands of years ago, a small stream developed with its origin in today's Town of New Castle, just north of the City of White Plains. This small river eventually emptied into the East River and, was called by the Native Americans Aquahung, a word that meant a place of high bluffs or banks. For centuries before the coming of the Europeans to New York the Native Americans used this pure, clean river for transportation and fishing, in addition to hunting along its banks. Joseph Rodman Drake (1725—1820), who has been recognized as the poet of the area, frequently rowed and fished in what became known as his beloved Bronx River. One of his poems painted a picture of a beautiful, clean river, with green banks on either side.

> I sat me down upon a green bank side,
> Skirting the smooth edge of a gentle river,
> Whose waters seem unwillingly to glide,
> Like parting friends who linger while they sever
> Enforced to go, yet seeming still unready
> Backward they wind their way in a many wistful Eddy.

By the early 1970s Drake's beautiful river, along whose banks he wished to be buried, had become polluted. Near its banks ran a highway and unsightly train tracks. The water was dirty with life—destroying sewage deposited by a population of people who did not care or were unaware of the rapidly increasing pollution of the Bronx River.[18]

"The Bronx River Project" was based upon a well—organized plan and a basic premise. The plan was to gather data on the stretch of the Bronx River within The New York Botanical Garden. A little less than a mile of the River is contained within The Garden. "The Project" was designed to gather every possible bit of information and data on the River within The Garden. The premise was that our earth was arranged under numerous environmental systems, within which there were regional systems and then sub—systems. The Bronx River, itself, was one of five rivers that entered the New York City area from the north. The Bronx River, in turn, was broken down into various subsystems as it flowed from the Kensico Reservoir area north of the City of White Plains and emptied into the East River in the Bronx. The stretch of the Bronx River within The Garden was one sub—system and was marked by the Project for a minute examination and the gathering of data. If this section of the River was better understood, then the entire River was better known. This understanding then provided a better knowledge of the area's water systems and contributed to furthering the comprehension of the entire planet's environmental system. "The Bronx River Project" concentrated on the micro—system within The Garden, the understanding of which helped to enlighten researcher's concept of the macrocosm.[19]

The procedure of amassing information and data on the Garden—enveloped sub—system of the Bronx River began in the Spring of 1973. Among the group of information gatherers were twelve students chosen from four nearby high schools: Theodore Roosevelt, Evander Childs, Christopher Columbus and the Bronx High School of Science; the number of high school participants eventually rose to twenty—four. All students received academic credit for their participation and were chosen by their schools for their scholastic aptitude and specific interests in the project. Thus, the participants benefited by their participation, while helping to solve the earth's environmental problems. The Garden thus afforded the students the opportunity to learn vital lessons in problem solving and to become aware of the delicate nature of the planet's environment.

Groups of students worked under a Garden representative who had expertise in various areas, thus providing the students with direction and a resource person. To get away from the classroom atmosphere, each student was permitted to select an area of study based upon his or her particular interest; all choices, of course, based upon the premise of making a complete study of the Bronx River. Students interested in biology and chemistry worked together on water analysis, temperature of the water and the atmosphere, nutrient contents of the river and fish, plant and animal life within the River itself and along its banks. Students interested in photography spent their time taking photos of both banks in order to provide a visual resource for the final analysis of the River. Other groups dealt with the archeology, history and mapping of the River, while some concerned themselves with civil law to deal with the legal ramifications of disturbing the Bronx River when clean—up operation began and steps were taken to keep it free of pollution.[20]

By the Spring of 1974 the in—depth investigation had revealed interesting, but disturbing, facts and conditions about the waterway. The students had found oil and gasoline on the surface, pipes discharging harmful chemicals and objects such as the remnants and complete bodies of cars and discarded refrigerators——all the result of a careless, environmentally—ignorant, contemporary society. Scientific analysis of the water had demonstrated very significant levels of contaminating bacteria and the presence of nitrates and phosphates that threatened all forms of life in the River.

The students did not confine themselves only to an investigation of the Bronx River within the confines of The Garden. One six—mile investigative journey into Westchester County revealed twenty—nine pipes emptying waste into the waters that eventually flowed through the section of the River within The Garden. Near the Cross County Parkway in Westchester County there were a number of active sewers and near 233rd Street in the Bronx two especially large, operative sewers spewing pollutants. As the River flowed through The New York Botanical Garden and The Bronx Zoo very little waste was added to the water. At 180th Street, however, there began an almost indescribable amount of contamination. From this point southward the students found the following: food store's daily deposited their garbage, hundreds of discarded box springs, bicycles, shopping carts, rubber tires and even one Volkswagon automobile. South of 180th Street was an environmentalist's nightmare where the waste of American urban society was in full view.

The students examining the history of the Bronx River discovered that in

1906 the Governor of New York signed a bill establishing a commission to explore the problem of the increasing pollution of the waterway. This was in response to the complaints of the odor and waste that disturbed communities and people along the River. The commission eventually recommended that the construction of a landscaped parkway along the waterway would greatly alleviate the problem. This parkway, along with turning control of access to the Bronx River over to local municipalities along the River, would eliminate the pollution coming from homes, small shacks and mills, so stated the state commission. At a cost of over sixteen million dollars the Bronx River Parkway was finally completed in 1925. Neither suggestion by the 1906 Commission solved the pollution problem, but instead obviously made it worse, as "The Project" was discovering.[21]

"The Bronx River Project", however, reported that the situation was not hopeless. The members reported that in spite of all of the depredations made upon the River, nature was persistent and was trying to make a comeback. "Myriad life forms have been found clinging tenaciously to what is left of their battered habitat". Near the Snuff Mill the bottom rocks were covered with algae. Diatoms and small invertebrate cyclops were collected. Minnows, which live upon these tiny life forms, were found in the shallows of the River. The pollution—resistant carp imported from China toward the end of the nineteenth century were still present and, in fact, were foraging on the waste—covered river bottom, thus doing nature's part in trying to clean the Bronx River of contamination.[22]

The goals of "The Bronx River Project" were many and varied. First, The Garden collected the data to make decisions to protect the small portion of the waterway within its environs. Second, the Bronx community was provided with information to correct over—crowding conditions that were contributing to pollution. Third, the various environmental protection agencies of the government had information to understand and to act upon the crisis facing this one small portion of the State of New York. Fourth, other areas of the nation had a model to use to obtain information and take steps to reverse pollution. The data and conclusions on the state of the Bronx River were a message that the Chicago River, Lake Erie and other environmentally damaged waterways had similar problems, yet were not beyond repair. The main goal of "The Project", however, was to clean—up the Bronx River. The waste from sewers must be terminated; discarded automobiles, tires and other such debris must be removed; accumulated garbage and waste must be cleaned up; and the careless living habits of people must be changed. Based upon the data, analysis and suggestions coming from "The Bronx River Project", the proper authorities and influential people now had the information to take steps to clean up and to save the Bronx River from total environmental destruction.[23]

Chapter XI: The Conservatory, Library, Herbarium

A botanical garden has three distinct entities. In the first place, it has facilities for indoor and outdoor plantings. At a botanical garden the indoor facility is called a conservatory. Secondly, a botanical garden possesses a very fine library and thirdly, it has a herbarium where dried plants are stored. Within twenty years of its foundation in 1895 The New York Botanical Garden possessed one of the largest botanical museums (which included the library) in the world, the largest conservatory in America and one of the largest collections of herbaria in the United States. In the decades since the early part of the twentieth century The Garden increased the quality of its facilities and the notoriety of its reputation in these areas.

In spite of all the accomplishments and prestige of The New York Botanical Garden, The Conservatory by the 1960s was in need of extensive repairs. In fact, by the early 1970s the deterioration of the complex was such that repairs, no matter how extensive, were not sufficient to save The Conservatory. The Garden staff realized that it would soon be forced to demolish the "Crystal Palace"; only a complete restoration project could save what Nathaniel Lord Britton in 1906 called "one of the most elegant buildings of its kind in the world".

Built in 1899, opened to the public in 1900 and completed in 1902, The Conservatory's statistics were best described in superlative terms, starting with a great glass dome over 90 feet high. The enclosed space measured 1,287,390 cubic feet; the glass area is 91,750 square feet with 17,000 panes of glass; the covered ground area is 50,272 square fee, or about 1.15 acres. When completed, The Conservatory was divided into fifteen chambers with complex methods of machinery to control and alter heating, shading and ventilation, in order to satisfy the needs of various types of plant life. This elaborate system was able to create the conditions analogous to various areas of the planet such as the desert, rain forest and the temperate zone. Placing emphasis upon the diversity of plant life throughout the planet, eventually more than six thousand plants were exhibited in pots, tubs and boxes on the floors and arranged in orderly rows. With a work force of more than twenty full—time gardeners, painters, glaziers and plumbers, The Conservatory superbly served the staff, scientists and the general public for more than thirty—seven years without major repair work.[1]

In 1937, when relinquishing more than one hundred acres of property for the construction of the Bronx River Parkway, The Garden lost the smaller Guggenheim Conservatory, referred to as Range No.2. This loss placed greater importance and use upon the larger Range No.1, which was showing its age and in need of renovation. This conservatory was closed, partially disassembled, repaired and opened once again in 1939. Plantings were no longer in tubs and pots, but in uniquely prepared ground with the surroundings typical of the native environment of the plants. In the selection of plants, emphasis was put upon species from the warmer parts of the planet.

In the years following the renovations made in the late 1930s various factors brought a decline in the condition of the conservatory. The conservatory's deterioration, which was brought about by factors beyond the control of The Garden, was caused by the following factors: shortages of labor and material during World War II, and then post war conditions of inflation and recession and environmental problems. In 1953 the City of New York did some overhaul of the structure. However well intentioned, the City's efforts did not halt the continuing decay of The Conservatory. In 1972, therefore, the Board of Managers of The Garden decided to make major renovations on The Conservatory and to prepare new programs for the facility. The cost of the project was estimated at that time to be about $2.5 million, divided into $1.5 for deferred maintenance and restoration and $1 million for new presentations and exhibits.[2]

Enormous problems, some unforeseen, had surfaced, however, long before the momentous decision by the Board of Managers in 1972. In the first place, the greenhouses, themselves, had begun literally to collapse as early as 1960. Dr. Howard S. Irwin, the President of The New York Botanical Garden in the 1970s, described the condition of The Conservatory as very poor as early 1960, when he was hired as a research botanist. His description of the physical state of the facility in 1960 was as follows:

> The heating system leaked terribly. There were plumes of steam rising up everywhere. Ventilators on all the chambers were stuck shut. They were made of Florida cypress from the Everglades, an excellent wood for the purpose, but the dowels which held them together were made of a wood that rotted, so we didn't dare open them.
>
> Thermostats didn't work. The desert house was always too cold and the palm was always roasting. There were frequent electrical shorts and small fires, owing to the inroads of humidity and insects eating insulation off the wires. Over the years, the kinds of plants that could live under these conditions diminished, and the greenhouses became overgrown with the tough nuts that could survive. It all became just one big tunnel through amorphous verdure.

In the years after 1960, conditions, according to Irwin, became downright dangerous for visitors because glass panes started to fall. The screws in the strips that maintained the glass in position were corroding. He related that by the late 1960s The Garden authorities had to close The Conservatory

> whenever there was a high wind because so much loose glass fell in. We just sort of had our thumb in the wind all the time, and if it was blowing very hard we'd close. People never knew whether we were going to be open or not.[3]

The next major obstacle was to convince the Board of Managers that a major overhaul of the conservatory, followed by a complete restoration, was absolutely necessary. The great hindrance to such a decision by the Board was that the cost of such a project was enormous. The Board of Managers, for the most part, was comprised of lawyers, bankers and business people who lived in Manhattan's affluent East Side; many of them were disinclined to spend a great deal of money on a "greenhouse", as some of them thought of the Conservatory. President Irwin fortunately was able, at least, to convince a sufficient number of the Board members to authorize a professional study of the proposed project. With this authorization in hand a consulting firm was invited to make engineering and feasibility analyses to establish the cost of such necessary work. The cost was at least $2.5 million, this for a structure that originally was constructed for $180,300. The fact that this initial cost was for work at the turn of the century and that by the 1970s construction costs and inflation had drastically changed the situation apparently did not enter the minds of many board members. Most of them were shocked. One notable board member exclaimed: "Why don't we just take all the glass off and let vines grow, and it will make a fine arbor?"[4]

Howard Irwin realized that The Conservatory was one of the great attractions of The New York Botanical Garden. For the people of New York City, especially those living in the Bronx, the "Crystal Palace" was not only fascinating to visit, but was also an outstanding visual landmark. Whereas most of the Board members lived in the very prosperous East Side of Manhattan and had very little contact with the ordinary citizens of the City, Irwin had recently moved into a stone cottage on the grounds of The Garden. He now had the personal opportunity to meet visitors to the grounds and also began to attend the meetings of local civic organizations. As a result of his personal investigation the President discovered that

> We didn't really know how the community felt. But we were at a time in our institutional history and social evolution when it was obvious that institutions were going to have to go out into the community and serve community needs, not just sit here as bastions of privilege and say, come see us.

He concluded that "It was quite clear that if the Conservatory were allowed to go down, the Garden's reputation would never survive it. Despite its decay, that building was looked on as the orb of the Bronx. It had to survive". Irwin's dogged, painstaking determination, plus the prodding of Edward Larrabee Barnes (The Garden's architect) and the delicate digs of Ada Louis Hustable (architecture critic of *The New York Times*) finally persuaded the Board in late 1972 to make the decision to go ahead with the plans not only to save the great facility but to restore and improve The Conservatory.[5]

The next great hurdle was that President Howard Irwin had to raise the money for the project, for which there was no great rush of contributions. In early 1975 the City of New York agreed to pay for one half of the restoration, with the stipulation that the contribution from the municipality was not to exceed $1.5 million. The offer had hardly been made when it was withdrawn. The City, verging on bankruptcy, was forced to "defer" its partial subsidization of the project. In spite of the absence of large donations and the reversal of New York's offer, The Garden, certainly with more boldness than conviction, decided to proceed with the project. The undertaking, however, had to proceed with backing, not from the public sector, but from private donations.

Carlton Lees, formerly chief executive officer of the Pennsylvania and Massachusetts Horticultural Societies, was hired to direct the restoration project. On May 1, 1975, The Garden held a grand ball in the now derelict Conservatory. Lees laid down turf and filled the dome with flowers to establish a garden—like atmosphere amidst the early construction work. When the rains came that evening, the workmen covered the gaping holes in the ceiling with plastic, without complete success. Lees noticed that people avoided certain spots on the floor because the roof was leaking. In spite of the leakage the formal affair was a success, attracting people who were capable of contributing to the project. In fact, the 450 people in attendance realized first hand the need to restore The Conservatory to its former grandeur, and even to improve upon the services it could provide to science and to the general public. This vital work, however, required large sums of money. The first major contribution was obtained through the instrumental efforts of Mrs. Paul Mellon, who had attended the affair and later secured from the Mellon Foundation a $500,000 grant.

Contributions arrived from various sources, but expenses for the restoration increased, along with inflation. Gradually the cost began to exceed the ability of The Garden to provide the necessary funds. For example, as the work proceeded, it was discovered that the condition of the great dome was far worse than envisioned. At social gatherings of the staff and associates of The Garden the topic of conversation, of course, was invariably the restoration. One evening Carlton Lees was asked why he had not first commenced work on the great dome, the centerpiece of The Conservatory. Lees' answer was that "The dome will take care of itself. If we do it house by house and skip the dome and go on to the rest, it will be so obvious that someone will come forward". This inquiry concerning the dome, was made by Mrs. Enid Haupt, a member of the wealthy and influential Annenberg family, one time publishers of the magazine *Seventeen*. She had donated to several gardens but had exhibited little interest in the New York Botanical Garden, especially in the restoration of The Conservatory. That evening, however, Mrs. Haupt donated $850,000 for work on the great dome.[6]

Sometime later Howard Irwin, Carlton Lees and several other garden executives were invited for lunch at Mrs. Haupt's Park Avenue apartment. The expense of the restoration work had increased from $2.5 million to $4 million, with the cost expected to rise even higher. The Garden group arrived at her lavishly furnished apartment expecting to be criticized as poor business men for allowing the cost to reach a level that very likely doomed the project to failure. Instead, Mrs. Haupt surprised everyone to the point of speechless shock by offering to pay for the entire restoration of the Conservatory, regardless of the cost. She believed that this work was vital to the people of the City of New York and to the world's scientific community. The great importance of the work justified nothing less than Mrs. Enid Haupt's complete support of the project.

With the entire restoration assured by Mrs. Haupt's gift, the attention of Carlton Lees and the staff turned from structural work to the ornamental details of the structure, aspects of the project that had been given a low priority. The decision to restore the decorative trimmings in turn created problems. First, Lees needed the original plans, which proved to be lost and thus unavailable. He even went so far as to search through the archives and records of New York City's Parks Department. Without the original plans the architect, Edward L. Barnes, thus decided to re—create from some old photographs the original ornamental castings, a type of decorative work that had flourished in the United States during the period from about 1860 to 1890, but which was becoming outdated by the time that The Conservatory construction was completed.

The next problem was the search for a professional expert in nineteenth century restoration work, someone who was capable of making intricately detailed illustrations from the old photographs. With the drawings completed by an architectural historian, attention was turned toward finding a woodcarver capable of making molds for ornamental cast iron; there were some 12,000 intricately detailed, decorative segments that had to be made. To discover such an "artist" proved to be a long and nation—wide search, for specialists of this type were indeed rare. Finally, in Salt Lake City, Utah, was found a woodcarver named Ron Rumel whose family business went back to the time of Brigham Young. An ancestor had spent an entire lifetime on the intricate details involved in the construction of the Morman Temple in Salt Lake City. Rumel was quite able to carve the elaborate wooden patterns and a Utah foundry made the exquisitely beautiful castings, using aluminum instead of iron. [7]

The Conservatory reopened on March 18, 1978, after having been closed to the public for two years to complete the necessary renovations. The Italian Renaissance—style "Crystal Palace" was renamed the "Enid Haupt Conservatory of the New York Botanical Garden". The Garden announced that Mrs. Haupt's offer to pay for the entire restoration amounted to a gift of about $5 million, which included the previously bestowed gift of $850,000 in 1976. The donations made by other benefactors were shifted, with the consent of the donors, to other projects such as the collection and design of the horticultural displays within the Enid Haupt Conservatory.

Carlton Lees used his inventive genius in creating the various display areas, with each airy space possessing a unique theme. There was an American desert, as well as an "old world" desert; a fern forest with a waterfall; space for subtropical plants; and sections to arouse the interest of children. In the children's greenhouse, called "Greenmuse", on opening day there was a special theme called "grocery store botany". On simulated grocery store shelves there were cans of tomato soup and other vegetables. Nearby there were the corresponding plants so that the children were able to connect the finished products with the growing plants. Downstairs there were rooms where lectures on the basics of plant life were offered by staff members to the children of the local schools.

There were sections devoted to mosses, aquarium plants, mushrooms and ordinary house plants growing under artificial light. In one garden space there was a bay tree encircled by a seat constructed of turf. This was something found in medieval gardens and was used by the ladies of the castle. Nearby was a landscape called parterre, with dwarf boxwood cultivated in scrolls and swirls, which were also part of the garden of a medieval castle. The magnificent central dome was devoted to the palms and had a special appeal for visitors who were attracted to the height of the great trees. Throughout the Conservatory there were no longer lengthy, straight walkways, but rather pathways that wandered in and around the plants, trees and displays. Carlton Lees explained his intention was to have people "meander" through the Conservatory, rather than "walk" through the horticultural exhibitions.

Mrs. Enid Haupt summed up the importance of the restoration project and her involvement with the following sentiment.

> Restoration of this beautiful complex has been a marvelous experience. Growing flowers and living with nature enhances life enormously. It gives me great satisfaction to share this philosophy with the public.[8]

Over the years Enid Haupt's philanthropy has provided thousands of people the pleasure of seeing her sentiments enshrined in various permanent collections, numerous valuable specimen plants and constantly changing displays of plants, flowers and trees.

Nathaniel Lord Britton in his "Report of the Secretary and Director—in—Chief for the Year 1904" remarked that

> We should certainly aim to make the library as complete as possible in
> pure botany, and in its related sciences of horticulture, agriculture,
> forestry, and such portions of general biology as apply to plants and I
> believe that no greater service could be rendered to these subjects in
> America than by some provision by means of which our library should
> be perfected.

Britton's comments became the basic philosophy and modus operandi of
The Garden's Library down through the decades. In addition, not mentioned by
the founding director, but a condition of equal importance was that the contents
and facilities of the library were always readily available for research to members
of both the scientific community and the general public. From its inception,
therefore, the library has not only served as a depository of knowledge, but also a
place for qualified and interested students to retrieve that information.[9]

From the time of the founding of The New York Botanical Garden in 1895
the goal was to develop the library into one of the great research facilities of its
kind in the world. In the same year of the foundation of The Garden the prestigious Columbia University (founded as Kings College in 1754 by the royal charter
of his majesty King George II of Great Britain) agreed to place its entire botany
collection on permanent loan to the library of the newly established institution.
Both institutions agreed that the goal was to develop the new library into one of
the great botanical research centers in the world. As part of the agreement the
books on "loan" were available to Columbia faculty and students for research and
were subject to recall if needed. In 1899 the Columbia collection of about 5,000
books was transferred and soon interfiled with 2,500 volumes already in the
possession of The Garden. From this modest collection the library by 1969 had
expanded to more than 80,000 books and 315,000 unbound monographs, pamphlets and reprints.

From time to time The Garden continued to receive donations of valuable
books from Columbia University. In 1901 the University deposited 200 volumes
and 300 pamphlets from its paleobotany collection. In 1904 Columbia donated a
complete gift of titles of publications of state and horticultural societies; and then
there were many gifts of a smaller nature over the years. In 1899, New York
Hospital donated over 200 early editions of botanical books from the collection
gathered by Dr. David Hosack, the founder of the Elgin Botanic Garden, considered to be the forerunner of The New York Botanical Garden. In 1900 and in
1905 books from the New York Academy of Science (formerly the Lyceum of
Natural History and founded in 1817) were presented to The Garden through the
American Museum of Natural History. Over the decades there have been many
valuable gifts from individuals, such as from the private libraries of Nathaniel T.

Kidder, Sarah Gildersleeve Fife, Clarence McKay Lewis, Dr. Lerner D. Merrill and Dr. Norman Taylor. Photographs, slides, horticultural correspondence and a card index devoted to the study of Clematis were willed to The Garden from the estate of I. E. Spingarn.[10]

Donations of valuable books and collections were not the only means by which the library increased its holdings. A "Special Book Purchase Fund" was established very early in the history of The Garden. Interested people were encouraged to assist this fund with their financial contributions; the noted philanthropist, Andrew Carnegie, was an early contributor to this endowment. As early as 1902 Dr. Britton made the first major purchase from this fund when he acquired in Berlin, Germany, a valuable collection of 400 to 500 books depicting Pre—Linnean Botany and Natural History. In a Paris, France, auction over 500 books and pamphlets from the Alexis Jordan library were obtained; this purchase was largely made possible by a significant contribution from Andrew Carnegie.

In 1905 The Garden entered into an agreement with the company of J. Georg of Geneva, Switzerland, to purchase, as soon as they appeared for sale, all botanical works and collections printed between 1700 and 1870. This contracted agreement continued until the period of World War I. With the merger of several botanical establishments in Geneva, Switzerland, the largest single purchase by The Garden library (up to 1969) was concluded in 1923. This purchase consisted of duplicates from the newly—formed Swiss book depository and contained over 5,000 books and many thousands of pamphlets. The Garden paid $13,000 for this duplicate collection, which weighed over twelve tons and was so extensive that it took about ten years to be catalogued into the library's existing collection. In April, 1966, duplicates from the private, botanical library of Kenneth K. Mackenizie were bought from the Horticultural Society of New York. This acquisition, made as a result of a large donation from the Women's Council of The New York Botanical Garden, provided the library with a valuable collection of early works on botany.[11]

Almost from the foundation of The Garden the library has engaged in exchange programs with other organizations. This system of exchange became an effective means of increasing the holdings of the library, especially scientific journals, without significantly increasing expenditures. By 1969 the library had entered into some 800 exchange arrangements that brought over 1,200 serials to the library. This accounted for about one—half of the total number of serials acquired by the library at that time. The exchange program proved to be very effective in obtaining titles from areas of the world from which it was difficult to access any form of publication. For example, Exchange Number 244 was instituted with a mycologist in Romania. In exchange for American books, which this scientist could not purchase because of the Iron Curtain, she forwarded Eastern European publications that The Garden library had found difficult to obtain. Similar agreements were made with scientists in South America and the Union of Soviet Socialist Republics.

The Garden, and specifically the library, was founded to serve the scientific community and the general public. The library staff has devised various methods to accomplish these objectives. In the metropolitan area the library quickly became recognized as the finest research center for botanical and horticultural research. As a result, such institutions as the New York Public Library routinely directed questions and questioners of a botanical and horticultural nature to The Garden library. In 1968 there were more than 4,000 non—staff visitors doing some type of research. Also in 1968 there were about 2,500 requests for information from such areas as New York City, the State and Federal Government, publishers of scientific journals, authors, artists, engineers, and law firms. A librarian was usually assigned to answer the questions received by mail, telephone or in person.

The Garden library has never been a lending library but has entered into formal, interlibrary loan agreements with other institutions. In 1966 the library forwarded all catalog copy to the National Union Catalog at the Library of Congress. The library also has a policy of reporting all new acquisitions to the New Serials Titles office of the Library of Congress. Since 1966 the library has been involved in establishing the Union Catalog of Medical Periodicals at the Medical Library Center of New York, a computerized list of biological and medical periodicals. All of these efforts have made the holdings of the library better known and more accessible, thus participating in The New York Botanical Garden's mission to serve educators, researchers and the general public with botanical and horticultural information.[12]

By 1969 the Library had developed what was referred to as "Special Collections". This included such areas as the Charles Finney Cox Collection of Darwiniana, the Manuscript Collection and Archives, the Photographic Collection, the Reprint Collection, Seed Catalogs, Vertical Subject File and the Rare Book Collection. The Charles Finney Cox Collection is a sizable and significant number of books, pamphlets and other documents associated with Charles Darwin. Originally the collection was a private one assembled by Charles Cox, a founder and a treasurer of The New York Botanical Garden. As a hobby Mr. Cox had collected these items that The Garden purchased in 1912. Then, from time to time, additional items associated with Darwin were added by purchase. By 1969 the Cox collection comprised one hundred and twenty—five books (first editions, variant editions, foreign language translations of Darwin), various monographs on Darwin and Darwinism and one hundred and eighty five letters written by or to Charles Darwin.

The Manuscript Collection and Archives include a large assortment of documents and correspondence, including the abovementioned Darwin letters. These documents also contain over two thousand letters written to John Torrey (the founder of the Torrey Botanical Club) by various scientists during the nineteenth century. In addition, there are thousands of letters written by notable personages associated with botany; letters written by Noah Webster and Ralph

Waldo Emerson are included in this portion of the collection. In 1967 the historical archives of The Garden became part of the Manuscript Collection.

The contents and volume of the archives and manuscripts are truly extraordinary. The archives provide us with a history of The Garden since its foundation in 1891. It also incorporates works on the history of botany as a field of study. Included are unpublished documents and manuscripts such as the correspondence, field reports, photographs, maps, portraits and artifacts of many famous explorers, describing and illustrating their accomplishments. The contents of this collection boggles the mind when one learns that its length on the library's shelves extends nearly one mile.

The Photographic Collection consists of thousands of historical photos; at first they were not indexed. From 1935 to 1942 the United States government provided the services of workers from the Works Progress Administration (WPA) to index this large collection. Starting in 1942, however, little was done in the area of collecting and indexing photos. In 1962 this valuable indexing service was once again revived by the library, which then continued to add to and index the photo collection.

In the Reprint Collection the library maintains a valuable collection of reprints. This includes reprints of important journals, the monographs of important scientists and hard—to—find books that are not among the library's holdings. These reprints provide easy access to items not readily available to users of the library. Occasionally The Garden's Library was able to obtain the reprints of various collectors; included in these accessions were those valuable reprints of Dr. B. O. Dodge, Dr. R. A. Harper and Dr. Norman Taylor.

The library has amassed over the years a worldwide collection of seed catalogs and seed lists. The Garden's collection is not the largest in the United States, but it is the largest in the metropolitan area. The oldest catalogs date back to the mid—nineteenth century, while much older seed lists can be found in the library's main collection. Seed catalogs provide researchers with information on the history and development of various varieties of plants, as well as the story of garden designs and developments in the planning and establishment of lawns. These facts are important for historical societies, museums and anyone engaged in restoration work. The vertical file provides easy, quick access to information contained in newspaper clippings, photographs, biographical data and pamphlets, mainly dealing with the development of The Garden.[13]

The Rare Book Collection of The Garden consists mainly of books and manuscripts dating from before 1700; and some are dated from before 1500, which places them in an interesting and lovely classification of incunabula. This collection of rare and valuable works .was designed for historical and bibliographical purposes, rather than everyday research and study. The latter type of book is located in the main collections of the library. The Rare Book Collection includes "incunabula, herbals, and the works considered to be among the foundations in the field of botany, biology, materia medica, horticulture and gardening, and agriculture". Exceptions to the 1700 age limit were made in regard to "several nineteenth—century botanical works interleaved and annotated by John Torrey, some bound manuscripts, and a few important association copies".[14] The Rare Book Collection of the library, therefore, contains many treasures in the general field of botany.

In 1976 an extremely valuable addition was made to the Rare Book Collection. The Garden acquired "Circa instans", two rare manuscripts, so rare that they are considered the equivalent of the Dead Sea Scrolls. In spite of their importance these manuscripts have no title, simply because they received none from the author. The title given to them comes from the first two words of the manuscripts, "Circa instans", which means "about the present". The New York Botanical Garden was able to purchase these invaluable manuscripts through many private donations, the major contributors included Mrs. Enid Haupt and the Samuel H. Kress Foundation.[15]

"Circa instans" dates from the Middle Ages; the copies in the possession of The Garden are referred to as Manuscript A and Manuscript B by the institution. The former is presumed to be an earlier version, while the latter is a finer example of the calligraphy of that period. There is no title and no author simply because at that time such information was considered superfluous and thus unimportant. The important matter "was not who had done what, but how well it had been done". In today's world, however, such information is very important; and in the case of "Circa instans" the author and publication date can be reasonably ascertained. The author of "Circa instans" was almost certainly Matthaeus Platearius, the finest teacher at the Salerno, Italy, Medical School. This school was founded about 980 AD. and was the first such institution of its kind in Europe. The institution trained doctors in the prescription of drugs and in surgical procedures, for which doctors were also instructed in the use of anesthetics. The original "Circa instans" was written about 1140—1150 AD.[16]

The "Circa" is very valuable for a number of reasons. In the first place, it provides the modern world with an abundance of facts about the study of botany. At that time, most drugs used by physicians were herbals; thus botany, pharmacology and medicine were very closely related. The "Circa" thus yields information on twelfth century botany that almost cannot be secured from any other source. Secondly, it performed a great service for physicians at that time by eliminating a great deal of confusion about various medicines. Obsolete and duplicate names for various medicines were removed. The multitude of names had developed with the gradual introduction of the various forms of the vernacular, in place of Latin. The "Circa" also gave a description for each drug, with instructions for its application, thus aiding physicians in the use of the various medications. Although undoubtedly composed by Platearius, the "Circa" was the consensus of opinion of the "faculty" at Salerno. With its great tradition, medical experience and reputation European physicians placed a considerable amount of faith in the Salerno School's published opinions.

Even more importantly, the "Circa" introduced a break with the ancient classical past. For centuries the "medical profession" had accepted, as the definitive word, Dioscorides' *De Materia Medica* and Pliny's *Historia Naturalis,* both produced in the first century A.D. The Salerno School produced the first post—classical treatise on medicine and also dealt with medical problems never faced in the first century. In addition, in the twelfth century Europeans were coming into contact with the Islamic World where the medical profession was far ahead of Europe. There were new ideas and procedures, many of which were useful, yet were not found in Dioscorides and Pliny. At this time, Europeans also began to question, to abandon blind acceptance and to rely upon the personal experience of testing and observation; thus began the modem scientific method. All of these factors add to the significance of the "Circa instans".

The manuscript copies of "Circus instans" in The Garden library are rare and very old. *The Incunabula in American Libraries* for 1975 listed only thirteen printed copies in the United States, plus the manuscript copy in The Garden, making a total of fourteen in America. The New York Botanical Garden copies came from the library of the late Dr. Emil Starkenstein, formerly professor of pharmacology and pharmacognosy (the science of drugs) at the University in Prague. He also was a noted collector of the finest works related to the history of botany and pharmacology. Both Starkenstein copies of the "Circa" are on vellum (a fine kind of parchment prepared from calfskin, lambskin or kidskin) and are slightly different in minor details. This is understandable when one realizes that these manuscripts were copied by hand at different times and by different individuals. Their accuracy to details thus depended upon the attention and ability of each scribe. Manuscript A dates possibly from the end of the twelfth century and Manuscript B possibly from the beginning of the thirteenth century. As of 1976 they were believed to be the oldest copies of "Circa instans" extant. The antiquity of these vellum copies makes them very important because people are usually fascinated by their age and condition. More importantly, however, The Garden copies are the closest, as far as is known, in age to the original which was written about 1140—1150 A.D. The New York Botanical Garden, therefore, possesses one of the critical works in the development and history of botany, medicine and pharmacology.[17]

By 1979 the herbarium collection of The New York Botanical Garden had grown to four million specimens of dried plants. Since 1968 The Garden's herbarium had been listed as one of the three largest in the United States, the other two were at the Smithsonian in Washington, D.C. and at Harvard University in Boston, Massachusetts. Established in 1891, the same year as The Garden, the herbarium instantly became the depository of two large, very important collections acquired in earlier times by Princeton and Columbia Universities. Very interestingly, and perhaps recognizing the great future importance of the institution, The New York Botanical Garden also was given the herbaria from the exploration of the Missouri and Columbia River areas by the famous Lewis and

Clark Expeditions of 1803 to 1806.[18]

By the end of the 1970s The Garden herbarium was acquiring each year about 900,000 additional specimens for its existing collection. Seventy percent of this total came from explorations made by staff members and students associated with the institution and the rest by means of exchange with other herbariums. The astounding number of additional plants each year had made it impossible for the staff to prepare all the dried plants and there was a significant number of rooms filled with unmounted specimens. The herbarium kept a close record of all staff and associate expeditions starting with the first in the State of Montana in 1897. Since then explorations had been conducted and specimens collected and sent to The Garden from such places as Venezuela, Peru, Brazil, French Guiana, Japan, Canada, Mexico, Russia, South America, Antarctica, Malaysia, India, China and even closer to home, from New York State.

The Garden herbarium has added to its collection by exchange, a program similar to that conducted by the library. When explorations were sent into remote areas of the world, specimens usually were collected in duplicate. One was kept by The Garden, the other sent to another part of the world where there was a herbarium seeking such a specimen and willing to exchange it on a one—for—one basis. In the period from 1976 to 1979 specimens were sent to one hundred and fifty institutions in forty—six states and to thirty—one countries throughout the world.

Since 1966 The New York Botanical Garden herbarium was the recipient of financial assistance from the National Science Foundation and had a policy of never charging researchers for the use of its collection. From 1968 to 1979 more than two hundred visiting scientists each year used the herbarium collection, some remaining for as long as a year doing their research. It further served the research and scientific community through a loan program. In the twenty years before 1979 more than a half million specimens had been loaned to other institutions.

The herbarium is primarily a research establishment, but during the 1970s it was increasingly consulted on various problems faced by diverse agencies. Police departments conferred with the staff when seeking answers concerning plant parts found at the scenes of serious crimes, such as murder. The United States Customs Service has called on the herbarium staff for advice on drug cases, even requesting that they serve as expert witnesses. Curators have been called by urban communities concerning serious cases of pollution and its effects upon plant life. The department was also called for its advice on the environmental impact of the building of the trans—Amazonian highway in Brazil. In 1979 Dr. Patricia Holmgren, the herbarium curator, remarked that

> Because of its massive volume, the breadth of coverage of the plant kingdom, and the concentrated regional coverage in areas of research and interest, The New York Botanical Garden herbarium has become a primary source of materials for botanical research throughout the

world.[19]

Chapter XII: Conclusion

Legally established in 1891 The New York Botanical Garden, with its 250 acres of property of unsurpassed beauty, has become one of the oldest and largest botanical gardens in the United States and one of the leading botanical institutions in the world. The time of its founding was momentous in the history and development of Western Civilization. The half century from the late 1860s to the beginning of World War I in 1914 witnessed the flowering of western culture. In economics, technology, politics, industry, the arts and sciences Western Civilization reached undreamed heights; this was especially true in America where there was unbelievable progress. The founding of The New York Botanical Garden in the late nineteenth century thus came at a time when the success of the venture was supported by world and national events.

In the late nineteenth century the United States was charged with enthusiasm, energy and was full of ideas. The American people were tremendously receptive to the cause of developing the greatness of the nation and the people. There was tremendous interest in anything that was new and innovative, especially in the area of scientific development. The inclination and feelings of the nation thus made this period of time very advantageous for the establishment of a botanical garden. The founders of The Garden wisely took advantage of this American climate of opinion by inserting into the 1891 Act of Incorporation (See Appendix A) the following promises and designs for the future:

> for the purpose of establishing and maintaining a botanical garden and museum and arboretum therein... for the collection and culture of plants, flowers, shrubs and trees, the advancement of botanical science and knowledge and the protection of original researches therein and in kindred subjects, for affording instruction in the same, for the protection and exhibition of ornamental decorative horticulture and gardening and for the entertainment of the people.

The population of New York City was increasing enormously and expanding very rapidly into the suburbs. The desire to provide a better life for the people of New York, especially those crowded into the tenements of Manhattan Island, prompted the City in 1884 to acquire thousands of acres of property in the Bronx for the development of park land. The merging of several large estates, including that of the Lorillard family, resulted in the formation of Bronx Park. The Lorillards, a great tobacco—producing family, were also very interested in horticulture and in maintaining the beauty of their great estate. It was not totally by accident, then, that the founders of The New York Botanical Garden, when given a choice of property by the City of New York, selected Bronx Park and a portion of that park land that had largely comprised the magnificently maintained and developed Lorillard estate. The foundation of a great botanical garden was thus firmly based on the horticultural interests of the Lorillard family.

The late nineteenth century in the United States witnessed the growth of great wealth and financial empires; it was known as the "gilded age". The men who amassed great fortunes also became interested in philanthropy. The "gilded age" thus produced and then prompted such wealthy and influential men as Cornelius Vanderbilt, Andrew Carnegie and John Pierpont Morgan to support, finance and take an active role in the foundation and development of The New York Botanical Garden.

In spite of all these favorable circumstances The New York Botanical Garden would not have been established without Nathaniel Lord Britton and his wife Elizabeth Gertrude Knight Britton . These two determined, talented individuals, who worked so well together as a husband and wife team, were the major forces behind the origin and development of The Garden. They continued to be the spirit of the institution long after their deaths, even down to the present day. They were inspired by a visit to the Royal Botanic Gardens at Kew. Upon their return to the United States the Brittons carried to fruition their desire for a botanic garden for New York and its inhabitants.

The Brittons knew what was needed and realized how to achieve this goal, in spite of enormous obstacles. Their vision extended far and they comprehended better than anyone else the importance of this garden for their generation and for posterity. They were a team possessed of high energy, which was tempered by a great deal of self discipline and self—sacrifice. They were fine leaders whose leadership techniques were time—honored. The Brittons worked themselves hard, sometimes to the point of exhaustion. They selected talented colleagues who shared their dream and were willing to sacrifice. They made few mistakes, for their goals and methods were clear to themselves and to those with whom they worked. Finally, the Brittons shared the work, laboring on the grounds to insure that their dreams came to fruition.

Nathaniel and Elizabeth Britton created The New York Botanical Garden, pointed the institution to its present greatness and gave it a charisma that has remained to the present day. The spirit of the Brittons enabled The Garden to meet various challenges down through the decades: early growth problems, the needs of World War I, the great depression of the 1930s, the demands of World War II and such recent problems as environmental pollution and various human maladies. What was said of The Garden by Director Hartzog of the National Park Service in 1967 when it was designated as a National Historic Landmark could also be declared of the Brittons: "The legacy of The New York Botanical Garden is knowledge, and its ideal is truth and service".

Appendix A

THE NEW YORK BOTANICAL GARDEN, 1891 ACT OF INCORPORATION
As Amended by Chapter 103 of the laws of 1894,
Approved March 7, 1894.
Amendments of 1894 printed in italics
Chapter 285.
AN ACT to provide for the establishment of a botanic garden and museum and arboretum, in Bronx Park, in the City of New York, and to incorporate The New York Botanical Garden for carrying on the same.
Approved by the Governor April 27, 1891. Passed, three—fifths being present.
The People of the State of New York, represented in Senate and assembly, do enact as follows:
Section 1. Seth Low, Charles P. Daly, John S. Newberry, Charles A Dana, Addison Brown, Parke Godwin, Henry C. Potter, Charles Butler, Hugh J. Grant, Edward Cooper, Cornelius Vanderbilt, Nathaniel L. Britton, Morris K. Jesup, J. Pierpont Morgan, Andrew Carnegie, Thomas F. Gilroy, Eugene Kelly, Jr., Richard T. Auchmuty, D. O. Mills, Charles F. Chandler, Louis Fitzgerald, Theodore W. Myers, William C. Schermerhorn, Oswald Ottendorfer, Albert Gallup, Timothy F. Allen, Henry R Hoyt, William G. Choate, William H. Draper, John S. Kennedy, Jesse Seligman, William L. Brown, David Lydig, William E. Dodge, James A Scrymser, Samuel Sloan, William H. Robertson, Stephen P. Nash, Richard W. Gilder, Thomas Hogg, Nelson Smith, Samuel W. Fairchild, Robert Maclay, William H. S. Wood, George M. Olcut, Charles F. Cox, James R. Pitcher, Percy R. Pyne, and such persons as are now, or may hereafter be, associated with them, and their successors, are hereby constituted and created a body corporate by the name of The New York Botanical Garden, to be located in the City of New York, for the purpose of establishing and maintaining a botanical garden and museum and arboretum therein, for the collection and culture of plants, flowers, shrubs and trees, the advancement of botanical science and knowledge, and the prosecution of original researches therein and in kindred subjects, for affording instruction in the same, for the prosecution and exhibition of ornamental and decorative horticulture and gardening, and for the entertainment, recreation and instruction of the people.
Sec. 2. Said corporation shall have all such corporate powers, and may take and hold by gift, grant or devise all such real and personal property as may be necessary and proper for carrying out the purposes aforesaid, and for the endowment of the same, or any branch thereof: by adequate funds therefore.
Sec. 3. Said corporation may adopt a constitution and by—laws; make rules and regulations for the transaction of its business, the admission, suspension of the associate members of said corporation, and for the number, election, terms and duties of its officers, subject to the provisions of this act; and may from time to time alter or modify its constitution, by—laws, rules and regulations, and shall be subject to the provisions of Title 3, of Chapter 18, of the first part of the Revised Statutes.
Sec. 4. The affairs of the said corporation shall be managed and controlled by a board of managers as follows: The president of Columbia College, the professors of botany, of geology and of chemistry therein, the president of the Torrey Botanical Club, and the president of the Board of Education of the City of New York, and their successors in office, shall be ex—officio members of said corporation and of the Board of Managers, *and be known as the Scientific Directors*; they shall have the management and control of the

scientific and educational departments of said corporation and the appointment of the
Director—in—Chief of said institution, who shall appoint his first assistant and the chief
gardener, and be responsible for the general scientific conduct of the institution. All other
business and affairs of the corporation, including its financial management, shall be under
the control of the whole Board of Managers, which shall consist of the Scientific Directors,
as herein provided, and of the Mayor of the City of New York, the president of the Board
of Commissioners of the Department of Public Parks, and at least nine other managers to
be elected by the members of the corporation. The first election shall be by ballot, and held
on a written notice of ten days, addressed by mail to each of the above—named incorporators, stating the time and place of election, and signed by at least five incorporators.
Three of the managers so elected shall hold office for one year, three for two years, and
three for three years. The term of office of the managers elected after the first election, save
those elected to fill vacancies in unexpired terms, shall be three years; and three managers
and such others as may be needed to fill vacancies in unexpired terms shall be elected
annually, pursuant to the by—laws of the corporation. The number of elective managers
may be increased by vote of the corporation, whose terms and election shall be as above
provided; *and members may from time to time be added to the Scientific Directors by a
majority vote of the Scientific Directors, approved by a majority vote of the whole Board of
Managers*. The Board of Managers shall elect from their number a president, secretary and
treasurer, none of whom or of the Board of Managers, save the secretary and *treasurer*
shall receive any compensation for his services. *Nine corporators shall constitute a quo-
rum at any meeting of the incorporators, but a less number may adjourn.*

5. Whenever the said corporation shall have raised, or secured by subscription, a sum
sufficient in the judgment of the Board of Commissioners of the Department of Public
Parks in the City of New York, for successfully establishing and prosecuting the objects
aforesaid, not less, however, than two hundred and fifty thousand dollars within seven
years from the passage of this act, the said Board of Commissioners is hereby authorized
and directed to set apart and appropriate, upon such conditions as to the said Board may
seem expedient, a portion of the Bronx Park, *or of such other of the public parks in the City
of New York north of the Harlem River in charge of the said Department of Parks as may
be mutually agreed upon between the said Board of Commissioners and Board of Managers of said corporation in lieu of Bronx Park*, not exceeding two hundred and fifty acres,
for establishing and maintaining therein by the *said* corporation a botanical garden and
museum, including an herbarium and arboretum, and for the general purposes stated in the
first section of this act. And the *said* Board of Commissioners is thereupon hereby, authorized and directed to construct and equip within the *said* grounds so allotted, according
to plans approved by them and by *said* Board of Managers, a suitable fireproof building for
such botanical museum and herbarium, with lecture—rooms and laboratories for instruction, together with other suitable buildings for the care and culture of tender or other plants,
indigenous or exotic, at an aggregate cost not exceeding the bonds hereinafter authorized to
be issued by the City of New York; the use of *said* buildings upon completion to be
transferred to *said* corporation for the purposes stated in this act. And for the purpose of
providing means therefore, it shall be the duty of the Comptroller of the City of New York,
upon being thereto requested by said Commissioners, and upon being authorized thereto by
the Board of Estimate and Apportionment, to issue and sell at not less than their par value
bonds or stock of the Mayor, Alderman and Commonalty of the City of New York, in the
manner now provided by law, payable from taxation, aggregating the sum of five hundred
thousand dollars, bearing interest at a rate not exceeding three per centum per annum, and

to be redeemed within a period of time not longer than thirty years from the date of their issue.

Sec. 6. The grounds set apart, as above provided, shall be used for no other purposes than authorized by this act, and no intoxicating liquors shall be sold or allowed thereon. For police purposes and for the maintenance of proper roads and walks, the said grounds shall remain subject at all times to the control of the said Board of Commissioners of the Department of Parks; but otherwise, after the suitable laying out of the same and the construction of proper roads and walks therein by the Department of Parks, the said grounds and buildings shall be under the management and control of the said corporation. The said grounds shall be open and free to the public daily, including Sundays, subject to such restrictions only as to hours as the proper care, culture and preservation of the said garden may require; and its educational scientific privileges shall be open to all alike, male and female, upon such necessary regulations, terms and conditions as shall be prescribed by the managers of those departments.

Sec. 7. This act shall take effect immediately.

Appendix B: Overview of The New York Botanical Garden

By 2000 The New York Botanical Garden had become one of the leading institutions of its kind in the world. Located in Bronx Park, New York City, on a 250 acre site that includes striking rock formations, wetlands, ponds, a cascading waterfall and a 40 acre primeval hemlock forest that at one time covered all of New York City.

On the grounds is the nation's most beautiful Victorian glass house, the almost one acre Enid A. Haupt Conservatory which houses spectacular plant collections from tropical and desert regions of the world. The Conservatory is so named because of the spectacular philanthropic endeavors of a great woman, Enid A. Haupt. She began her association with The Garden in 1975 with a $5 million gift for the restoration of the glass—domed conservatory that now bears her name. In the late 1990s she again contributed to repair and refurbish the Conservatory. In all, the now deceased Enid A. Haupt over the years contributed $25 million to The Garden as well as millions more for cancer patients, museums and the nearby Bronx Zoo. She passed to her eternal reward on October 25, 2005, at the age of 90. In the February, 2006, issue of the American Orchid Society Journal there is a wonderful, well deserved tribute to Mrs. Enid Haupt.

Other notable buildings include the Snuff Mill (c. 1840), a Stone Cottage (c. 1840), the Museum Building (1901), the Charles B. Harding Research Laboratory (1956), the Harriet Barnes Pratt Library Wing (1965) and the Jeanette K. Watson Administration Building (1972), the latter two are extensions to the Museum Building. In 1971 The Garden obtained in Dutchess County a 1,800 acre expanse of land, at which was established the Cary Arboretum for research.

Plant Collections

The plant collections of The Garden number about 12,000 species, gathered from all parts of the world. Included are various types of gardens and arboretums that have been established and developed over the years.

Specialty Gardens

The Peggy Rockefeller Rose Garden comprises 2,700 beautiful examples of this very popular plant.

The T. H. Everett Rock Garden is a 2.5 acre example of one of the finest gardens of its kind in the world.

The Native Plant Garden contains plants found in 11 different habitats of the northeastern portion of the United States.

The Arlow B. Stout Daylily Garden is named after a man who worked at The Garden for almost four decades. Stout's specialty was the breeding of daylilies, which interest led him to the creation of dozens of new hybrids.

The Jane Watson Irwin Perennial Garden is a half—acre plot of perennials noted for their flowers, texture and foliage.

The Nancy Bryan Luce Herb Garden has been recently designed by Penelop Hobhouse and contains 92 species of European and American herbs.

The Demonstration Garden Complex was designed to provide ideas for the home gardens of visitors.

The Chemurgic Garden contains plant species that can be grown for chemical, medical and industrial uses.

The Ruth Rea Howell Family Garden and Beth's Maze was established and designed to afford instruction and pleasure for children.

Special Collections and Bulb Displays

The Bulb Display contains over 100,000 bulbs (one of the largest in the world) of such species of plants as eranthis, crocus, anemone, iris, muscari, chionodoxa, galanthus and scilla.

The Daffodil Display contains more than 100,000 plants, one of the largest collections of daffodils commercially available in the United States.

The Tulips. Annuals and Chrysanthemums are found at the Barbara Foster Vietor Walk, a path 270 feet long called the "reference library" of tulips, annuals and chrysanthemums.

The Sarah Davis Smith Orchid Collection contains more than 5,500 plants taken from approximately 650 species of orchids from Africa, Asia, the Caribbean, and Central, South and North America.

Irises and Peonies, found in flower beds on the northwest and east side of the Conservatory, contain 110 varieties of bearded iris and 58 types of herbaceous peonies.

Ferns, a collection considered to be one of the finest in the world, are hardy in temperate climates similar to New York City.

The Endangered and Threatened Plant Collection

Tree and Shrub Collections

Flowering Trees contain various species that bloom from April through June.

The NYBG Forest, containing a great assortment of birds and wildlife, is one of the oldest enduring examples of the natural woodlands that at one time covered New York.

The Montgomery Conifer Collection and Other Evergreens cover eight acres of exotic and native conifers.

Other Notable Trees, found in the area between the Museum Building and the Conservatory, include outstanding examples of the star magnolia, the Japanese pagoda tree, the sugar maple, tulip trees, Sargent's weeping hemlock, the Japanese yew, oaks and spruces.

Educational Programs

The Garden has always placed great emphasis and commitment to the area of public education, offering hundreds of programs in landscape design, commercial flower arranging and garden photography, all which attracted nearly 10,000 adults in the year 1993. To children of all ages are offered a wide range of classes, held every weekend afternoon from April to October. In addition, thousands of school children with their teachers visit The Garden throughout the year to participate in horticultural classes and tours. Starting in 1988, as part of its educational program, The Garden established the Bronx Green—Up Program to convert vacant lots into attractive working gardens. Since its inception this innovative program has been used in more than 170 communities in the Bronx.

The Botanical Science Division

This segment of The New York Botanical Garden has a staff of some 100 people, including 30 Ph.D. researchers. The mission of the B.S.D. is:

To carry out basic and applied plant research.

To share knowledge with the scientific community.

To organize, manage and make available the scientific assets of

The Garden

To train future botanists and enhance plant research throughout the world.

To attain these goals, the Botanical Science Division is arranged into eight departments as follows.

1) *The Institute of Systematic Botany (ISB)* documents, studies, researches and informs the scientific community about plant life throughout the world, with special emphasis upon plants in North, Central and South America and the Caribbean that are

threatened by environmental problems. Scientists and post—doctoral research associates conduct research projects and field activities in seven programs in the following seven geographic regions of the Americas: North America, Mexico & Central America, West Indies, Andes Mountains, Guayana, Amazon, and Planalto & Eastern Brazil. The ISB scientists then disseminate information on their findings through various NYBG publications, national and international seminars/meetings and the development of computerized databases of botanical information.

2) *The Institute of Economic Botany* (IEB) focuses its attention on the relationship between plants and people. The IEB is currently conducting field research in eighteen countries centering on the tropics. It studies natural resource management, conducts basic and applied research, explores the conservation of biological diversity, disseminates research findings, explores and teaches ways for the world community to enhance research in economic botany. Examples of the type and importance of IEB projects can be ascertained from the brief description of the following projects. One IEB activity is studying the ecology, administration and sale of fruits and other non—timber products in Indonesian Borneo. Another undertaking, this in the Central American nation of Belize, is identifying and studying plants used by the locals for food, clothing, fuel and medicine. The results of plant life studies in the last grouping are also being used by the National Cancer Institute in the battle against cancer and Aids.

3) *The Herbarium,* the underpinning of The Garden's research activity, currently contains more than 5.7 million specimens. It ranks fifth in the world, first in the Western Hemisphere and, in general, has been recognized in the international scientific community for its great significance. In existence for over one hundred years, its greatest strength is the collection of specimens from the Americas.

4) *The Library,* the basic instrument in support of the research efforts of the NYBG, holds more than 257,000 volumes of books and journals and more than one million non—book items. The Library holdings are strong in the following areas:
Literature on systematic botany from the fifteenth century onward;
Books on herbals from the 15th through the 17th Centuries;
Unpublished works, such as field collectors' notebooks;
Correspondence and papers of botanists and educators;
Administrative records of the NYBG;
Original botanical art.
In the Spring of 1994 the Library's on—line catalog, Catalpa, was introduced. Besides making easy access to users at the Library, Catalpa can be accessed on the Internet.

5) *The Harding Laboratory,* opened in 1957, conducts research and training in the broad areas of systematic and economic botany. Within this laboratory can be found the following areas of study and research:
Lewis B. and Dorothy Cullman Program for Molecular Systematic Studies;
Lieberman Laboratory conducts studies in systematic and developmental plant anatomy, histochemistry, cytology and palynology;
Mycological Laboratories feature research on fungal sytematics;
Phytochemical Laboratories employed for chemosystematic studies and for biodiversity studies, in conjunction with pharmaceutical companies;
A Scanning Electron Microscope Facility.

6) *Scientific Publications* fulfill an important function of The Garden's mission——the dissemination of research results and information to scientists throughout the world through a Publications Department. Begun in 1896, the publications of the NYBG

are unmatched throughout the world. Current serial titles include: *Advances in Economic Botany, The Botanical Review, Brittonia, Contributions from the NYBG, Economic Botany, Flora Neotropica, Memoirs of the NYBG, Mycologia* and *North American Flora.* The Garden also has published guides that have become standard reference works. Some of these publications are *Wild Flowers of the United States. The Evolution and Classification of Flowering Plants, Intermountain Flora* and *Index Herbariorum,* the latter is the directory of the world's herbaria.

7) *The Graduate Studies Program* is offered in conjunction with several area universities and gives students the opportunity to interact with various researchers, plus the use of The Garden's various research facilities. The NYBG also extends graduate fellowships in systematic and economic botany with stipends of slightly above $12,500 per year.

8) *The Lewis B. and Dorothy Cullman Program for Molecular Systematic* Studies, organizes and conducts molecular approaches in biodiversity research. Founded in 1994, the program is a joint initiative with The American Museum of Natural History. The goal of the Cullman Program is to strengthen research at The Garden to prepare for entry into the twenty—first century.

* * *The above represents a summary of some of the information found on The New York Botanical Garden on the World Wide Web.

Endnotes

Chapter I: History of Gardens

1. H. W. Rickett, "The Origin and Growth of Botanic Gardens", The Garden *Journal of the New York Botanical Garden (September/October, 1956, Vol. 6, #5), 133.*
2. Wolfgang Born, Ph.D., "Early Botanical Gardens", in Beate Caspari—Rosen, M.D., Editor, *Botanical Gardens* (Summit, New Jersey: Ciba Pharmaceutical Products Inc., 1949, 1099. Paper presented at a Ciba Symposium in July—August, 1949.
3. Ibid.
4. Ibid., 1101—1102.
5. Born, "Early Botanical Gardens", 1100—1101; Rickett, "The Origin and Growth of Botanic Gardens", 133; Nathaniel Lord Britton, "Botanical Gardens, Origin and Development", *Bulletin of The New York Botanical Garden* (January, 1897, I, 2), 62.
6. *Ibid.,* 1102.
7. There is still some controversy as to whether Padua or Pisa was first. The general opinion is that Padua takes precedence.
8. Rickett, "The Origin and Growth of Botanic Gardens", 135.
9. Born, "Early Botanical Gardens", 1102—1105.
10. Rickett, "The Origin and Growth of Botanic Gardens", 158—159.
11. Born, "Early Botanical Gardens", 1117.
12. Rickett, "The Origin and Growth of Botanic Gardens", 157.
13. Kenneth T. Jackson, *The Encyclopedia of New York City* (New Haven, Connecticut: Yale University Press, 1995), 559; David M. Ellis, *A History of New York State* (Ithaca, New York: Cornell University Press, 1967), 20; Ulysses Prentiss Hedrick, *A History of Agriculture in the State of New York* (New York: Hill and Wang), 85.
14. Jackson, *The Encyclopedia of New York City,* 559.
15. Hedrick, *A History of Agriculture in the State of New* York, 381.
16. Jackson, *The Encyclopedia of New York City,* 559.
17. *Ibid.,* 249; Henry H. Rusby, M.D., "A Historical Sketch of the Development of Botany in New York City", *Torreya* (June, 1906, Vol.6), 101. This is an address delivered before the Torrey Botanical Club on May 23, 1906, a copy of which is in the vertical file of the NYBG library.
18. Born, "Early Botanical Gardens", 1117; Rusby, "A Historical Sketch of the Development of Botany in New York City", 3—4; Jackson, *The Encyclopedia of New York City,* 559; "City's Old Botanical Garden", *The Evening Post,* January 5, 1901.
19. Nathaniel Lord Britton, "Botanical Gardens, Origin and Development", *Bulletin of The New York Botanical Garden* (January, 1897, I, 2), 62—63.
20. Frits W. Went, Ph.D., "The Broad Function of a Modern Botanical Garden", *The Garden Journal of The New York Botanical Garden* (July—August, 1961, II, 4), 126—127. Dr Went was the Director of the Missouri Botanical Garden and gave this address at a Members' Meeting of The New York Botanical Garden on February 28, 1961.

Chapter II: History of the Bronx River Area

1. Arthur Hollick, "The Geology of The New York Botanical Garden", *Journal of The New York Botanical Garden* (New York: Published for the Garden by the Science Press Printing Company, January, 1925), 3—6.
2. Up until 1874 all of the Bronx was part of Westchester County. In that year New York City annexed the Bronx towns of Morrisania, West Farms, and Kingsbridge. In 1888 New York City purchased the areas of Van Cortlandt, Crotona, Claremont, St. Marys, Bronx and Pelham Bay Parks; and Mosholu, Pelham and Crotona Parkways.
3. William Lawyer & Eliazbeth Betts Leckie, *Bronx River Retrospective: 300 Years Along the Bronx River Valley* (Scarsdale, New York: Published by the Greenburgh Nature Center & the Scarsdale Historical Society, 1983), 3—8.
4. Ibid. 9—10.
5.Gary Hermalyn, "A History of the Bronx River", *The Bronx County Historical Society Journal* (Bronx, New York: Published by The Bronx County Historical Society, 198?, XIX, 1), 2.
6.Lawyer and Leckie, *Bronx River Retrospective*, 10.
7. The story of the Lorillard tobacco enterprise on the Bronx River is taken in its entirety from an essay published by the author of this present monograph on the New York Botanical Garden. It is reprinted with gratitude and with the permission of the Westchester County Historical Society's Editor. See: Harry Dunkak, "The Lorillard Family of Westchester County: Tobacco, Property and Nature", *The Westchester Historian, The Quarterly of the Westchester County Historical Society* (Elmsford, New York: Published by the Westchester County Historical Society, Summer of 1995, Vol. 71, #3), 51—58.

Chapter III: Foundation

1. *New York Daily Tribune*, April 26, 1877; William J. Robbins, "Notes on the History of the Botanical Garden and Its Predecessors in New York City", *Journal of The New York Botanical Garden* (August, 1942, Vol. 43, #512), 201—205.
2. *New York Herald*, November 26, 1888.
3. *New York Herald*, November 27, 1888.
4. The Torrey Botanical Club was founded in 1867 by the noted botanist John Torrey (1796—1873), a pupil of the aforementioned David Hosack, who was a professor of botany and materia medica at Columbia College and the founder of the Elgin Botanic Garden. Torrey gained notoriety in 1817 by publishing a directory of plant life growing within thirty miles of New York City. In 1856 he was appointed a trustee of Columbia and given a residence in return for making available his significant library and herbarium to the College. In 1870 Torrey established the Bulletin of the Torrey Botanical Club, the first periodical on botany in the United States. See: Jackson (ed.), *The Encyclopedia of the New York City*, 130.
5. By 1888 Dr. Britton already had a long and distinguished teaching, research and publishing career at Columbia College. In 1887 he had been appointed Instructor in Botany and Geology at Columbia. Britton was married on August 27, 1885, to Elizabeth Gertrude Knight who also had an abiding interest in botany, especially the study of mosses. See: E. D. Merrill, "Biographical Memoir of Nathaniel Lord Britton 1859—1934", *National Academy of Sciences Memoirs* (Washington, D.C.: National Academy of Sciences, vol.

XIX, 1938), 147—159. Certainly there is a need for a lengthy biography of Nathaniel Lord Britton.

6. Merrill, "Biographical Memoir of Britton", 152; N. L. Britton, "History of the New York Botanical Garden, Read September 6, 1915, on the occasion of the Twentieth Anniversary Celebration", vertical files of the NYBG Library, 1—16; Frans Antoine Stableu, Unpublished manuscript on the very early history of the NYBG, contained in the vertical files of The NYBG Library, Chapter 2, 9; William J. Robbins, "The Founding of The New York Botanical Garden", *New York Botanical Garden Journal*, (January/February, 1952). Robbins relates that this committee "was a very distinguished and able group, varied in background but united by a common interest in plants". Sterns (1846—1926) was a noted amateur botanist; Hollick (1857—1933) was the long—time Curator of Paleobotany at The NYBG; Hogg (1820—1897) was a U.S. Marshall under President Lincoln and later served in Japan, both for the American and Japanese governments; Rusby (1855—1940) became Dean of the Columbia College of Pharmacy and later Curator of Economic Botany at The NYBG; Allen (1837—1902) was Dean of the Homeopathic Medical College in New York; Britton was professor of Botany at Columbia; Newberry (1822—1892) was Professor of Geology, Botany and Paleontology at Columbia and had been invited by Lincoln to membership on the committee organizing the National Academy of Sciences; Brown (1830—1913) was a judge of the U.S. District and later worked with Britton in publishing *Illustrated Flora of the Northeastern United States*.

7. "Torrey Botanical Club Appeal For a Public Botanic Garden in New York City", Files of The NYBG Library, This is a copy donated by Dr. H. A. Gleason.

8. *New York Commercial Advertiser* (January 15, 1889).

9. Robbins, "The Founding of the NYBG", 13.

10. Stafleu, unpublished mss. In The NYBG Library vertical files, Chapter 2, 10.

11. John Mullaly, "The New Parks Beyond the Harlem", (New York, prepared by John Mullaly, Commissioner of Parks, 1887), IX, X, 37, 38, 41. A copy of this report is contained in The NYBG Library.

12. "A Million—Dollar Garden", American Art Journal, February 23, 1889. From the vertical files of The NYBG Library, No author.

13. Stafleu, Chapter 2, 9—17.

14. *Ibid.*, 5—6.

15. See Appendix A for "The New York Botanical Garden, 1891. Act of Incorporation, As Amended by Chapter 103 of the Laws of 1894, Approved March 7, 1894". (Amendments of 1894 are underlined.). Copy found in the vertical files of the NYBG.

16. *Ibid.*, 7—8.

17. Britton, "History of The New York Botanical Garden", paper read in 1915, 2, Copy found in the vertical files of the NYBG.

Chapter IV: Early History

1. Low was the Mayor of Brooklyn from 1881 to 1885. In 1881 he also was elected to the board of trustees for Columbia College and became its president in 1890, remaining in that position until 1914. Low became a very active member of the Garden, supporting Britton's efforts administratively and financially.

2. Robbins, "The Founding of The New York Botanical Garden", 14; Charles P. Daly, "Want of A Botanical Garden in New York", Remarks given at a meeting held on May 19th, 1891; copy found in the vertical files of The NYBG Library.

3. At the same time Columbia promised to donate its herbarium collection to The Garden when it became operational.

4. Stafleu, unpublished manuscript, 13—18.

5. *New York Tribune*, February 26, 1893, The NYBG newspaper file.

6. The central position of Britton was concisely described by Doctor H. H. Rusby in the following statement.

> Doctor Britton's accomplishment in the establishment of our Botanical Garden is not likely to fail of appreciation by future generations, but they might easily fail to appreciate the difficulties attending such a vast work on such insufficient resources. Looking back on the conditions that confronted the enterprise, they seem appalling, and the undertaking hopeless—yet—here is the garden, just pride of a nation! None of the enthusiastic botanical band, with the exception of Judge Brown possessed enough means to justify even the starting of a subscription list, and but a very few of them had wealthy associates who might become interested. Again it was Doctor Britton who succeeded in inducing those few to initiate a campaign for funds. For years, the attempt persisted, but the work lagged and it was not until a determined group of women, led by Mrs. Britton, took to the warpath, that the minimum endowment of $250,000 was secured, and of this only the income might be used. Money for grading, road, path and bridge building, the location of lakes and the erection of buildings and conservatories, had still to be secured from the city administration.

See: E.D.Merrill, "Biographical Memoir of Nathaniel Lord Britton 1859—1934", 152.

7. *The Tribune* announced the names and sums as follows: J. Pierpont Morgan, $25,000; Columbia College, $25,000; Andrew Carnegie, $25,000; Cornelius Vanderbilt, $25,000; John D. Rockefeller, $25,000; D. O. Mills, $25,000; Judge Addison Brown, $25,000; William E. Dodge, $10,000; James A. Scrymser, $10,000; William C. Schermerhorn, $10,000; ex—Judge Charles P. Daly, $5,000; Oswald Ottendorfer, $5,000; Samuel Sloan, $5,000; George J. Gould, $5,000; Miss Helen M. Gould, $5,000; John S. Kennedy, $5,000; William Rockefeller, $5,000; James M. Constable, $5,000; Morris K. Jesup, $2,500; Mrs. Melissa P. Dodge, $1,000; Tiffany & Co., $1,000; Hugh N. Camp, $500.

8. *The New Daily York Tribune*, June 19, 1895.

9. Stafleu, Chapter 2, p. 24; Britton, "History of the New York Botanical Garden", 4; *The New York Daily Tribune*, August 1, 1895; Letter from the Assistant Secretary of the Department of Public Parks (Name is not legible) to N. L. Britton, dated August 3, 1895, Vertical Files of The NYBG.

10. *The New York Times*, August 18, 1895.

11. Stafleu, Chapter 2, 21—22; *The Evening Post*, March 7, 1896, The NYBG newspaper file.

12. Several people were considered, but Britton's qualifications easily made him the most desirable candidate. He had achieved noteworthy distinction as an author and teacher of Botany at Columbia. In addition, he had visited many European botanical gardens and

had an intimate knowledge and understanding of the foundation and development of The New York Botanical Garden. In fact, Britton (along with his wife, Elizabeth) was the prime mover "from its very inception", giving him a special "acquaintance with its peculiar needs and possibilities". Britton's appointment was unanimously approved by the Board of Managers, the appointment to take effect on July 1, 1896. See: *New York Sun*, May 22, 1896.

13. See: "An Assault on Bronx Park", *Harpers Weekly*, July 3, 1897; "A Glaring Case", *The Sun*, July 22, 1897; "No Bronx Museum Yet", *The Sun*, September 17, 1897; "Bronx Museum Funds", *The Mail and Express*, September 23, 1897; "Give Us The Botanical Garden", *New York Dispatch*, September 26, 1897; "Botanical Garden Bonds", *The New York Evening Sun*, September 29, 1897.

14. Some of the compromises were that the Garden Managers agreed to eliminate homes for the Director and Chief Gardener and to reposition the powerhouse and conservatory.

15. Timothy Rub, "The Institutional Presence in The Bronx", in *Building a Borough, Architecture and Planning in the Bronx, 1890—1940* (New York The Bronx Museum of The Arts, 1986), 93—97. Article contained in the vertical files of The NYBG Library.

16. The description of the original museum building is taken mainly from Rob Bernstein, "The NYBG Museum Building", *Garden Journal* (March/April 1985), 3—4; Also see: *The Evening Post*, June 25, 1898; *The Evening Post*, October 25, 1899.

17. "Heroic Statuary Gets Scrubbing Bath", "Newsletter of The New York Botanical Garden" (September—October 1968). The large marble basin was completed in 1899 and the statue installed in 1905. According to the article the merman and mermaid "gave up the 'Struggle for Existence,' and now rest quietly in the corner of a dark and dusty storehouse".

18. *The Sun*, July 23, 1899.

19. "Bronx Botanical Garden", *The York Times*, Sunday, August 19, 1900.

20. *"A Guide to the Conservatories"*, *Journal of The New York Botanical Garden (Vol. VII, #75, March, 1906), 51—53*.

Chapter V: Developments Down to the Depression

1. *The New York Times*, Sunday, November 11, 1900; N. L. Britton, "Report of the Director—in—chief on results of his trip to Europe, 1900", *Journal of The New York Botanical Garden*, (Vol. I, #12, December, 1900) 177—183.

2. "Growth of the Botanical Garden", *The Evening Post*, January 14, 1901.

3. "The Botanical Garden", *Commercial Advertiser*, May 26, 1900.

4. E. D. Merril, "Biographical Memoir of Britton", *National Academy Biographical Memoirs*, XIX, 154—156.

5. In the two previous summers Rydberg led collecting expeditions to Montana. He was funded by the Division of Agrostology of the United States Government. See: J. W. Blankinship, "A Century of Botanical Exploration in Montana", *Montana Agricultural College Science Studies* (Bozeman, Montana: Published by the College, Vol. I, #1, November 1, 1904), 13—14.

6. Per Axel Rydberg, Ph.D., *Memoirs of the New York Botanical Garden* (New York: Published by The New York Botanical Garden, 1900), vii—viii.

7. Carol H. Woodward, "Creator of Puffed Cereals —and Benefactor of Science", *Journal of The New York Botanical Garden* (vol. 44, #524, August, 1943), 173—180;

Alexander P. Anderson, "A New Method of Treating Cereal Grains and Starchy Products", *Journal of The New York Botanical Garden* (vol. III, #29, May, 1902), 87—89.

8. *The Evening Post*, March 15, 1902.

9. "Got Rare Botanical Library", *The New York Times*, September 21, 1902.

10. Britton, "History of The New York Botanical Garden", 7—10.

11. "Report of the Secretary and Director—in—chief for the Year 1902", *Bulletin of The New York Botanical Garden* (Vol. 2, #8, 1903), 418—419.

12. "Report of the Secretary and Director—in—Chief for the Year 1905", *Bulletin of The New York Botanical Garden* (Vol. 5, #15, 1906), 11.

13 "Report of the Secretary and Director—in—Chief for the Year 1906", *Bulletin of The New York Botanical Garden* (Vol. 5, #17, 1907), 207—208.

14 "Free Lectures at Botanical Garden", *Bronx Borough Record and Times*, Sunday, April 15, 1906, The NYBG newspaper file.

15. "Botanical Garden Work", *The Saturday Evening Post*, November 5, 1906, The NYBG newspaper file.

16. In 1937 The New York Botanical Garden agreed to release about 140 acres of land to the City of New York to construct a north to south   expressway to link the Triborough Bridge and the Westchester County parkway system. Specifically the new roadway was an extension of the Bronx River Parkway and would link Westchester with Queens and Manhattan. See: "Botanical Garden Aids New Highway", *The New York Times*, March 29, 1937, The NYBG newspaper file.

17. Britton, "History of the Botanical Garden", 10; "Grant, By The City, of the Use of Additional Land in Bronx Park", *Journal of The New York Botanical Garden* (Vol. XVI, No. 185, May, 1915), 85—89; "140 Acres Added to Bronx Garden", unnamed newspaper, April 15, 1915, The NYBG newspaper file.

18. "The New York Botanical Garden, The Rose Garden, 1916—1929", No Date, No Author, from The NYBG Vertical Files.

19. N. L. Britton, "The Rose Garden Plans", *Journal of The New York Botanical Garden* (Vol. XVII, #200, August, 1916), 111—115.

20. Vanessa Davy, "Roses at the Garden", *Garden Journal*, No date, 3—4, Vertical Files of The NYBG.

21. "Historic Flower Garden Restored with $1 million Rockefeller gift", A newspaper article, with no author, no date and no sources, from the Vertical Files of The NYBG.

22. H. A. Gleason, "The Iris Garden", *Journal of The New York Botanical Garden* (Vol. XXIV, #283, July, 1923), 140—141.

23. *Journal of The New York Botanical Garden* (Vol. XIX, #223, August, 1918), 185—187; Marshall A. Howe, "The Dahlia Border", *Journal of The New York Botanical Garden* (Vol. XIX, #227, 1918), 291—292.

24. Kenneth R. Boynton, "The Narcissus Collection", *Garden Journal of The New York Botanical Garden* (Vol. XXV, #300, December, 1924), 320—322.

25. Elizabeth G. Britton, "The Rock Garden," *Garden Journal* (Vol. XXVIII, #331, July, 1927). 168—171.

26. The rock garden is named after Dr. W. Gilman Thompson, one of the Garden's earliest supporters and administrators; Scientific Director from 1896 until 1901; member of the Board of Managers from 1902 to 1926; and President of the Botanical Garden from 1913 until 1922. His horticultural interests centered on native plants, England. When Thompson died in 1927, he bequeathed to the Garden especially those of New York and also $5,000, which was used to start the rock garden named after him.

27. T. H. Everett, "The Thompson Memorial Rock Garden", *Journal of The New York Botanical Garden* (Vol. XXXIII, #395, November, 1932), 256—257; Mary W. Kenneth, "The Thompson Memorial Rock Garden", *Garden Journal* (May/June 1968), 94—96.

28. Ruth Caviston, Unpublished manuscript on the history of the Botanical Garden, catalogued in The NYBG Library, 89—91.

29. Remsen Crawford, "Wild Plants as War—Time Vegetables", *Collier's Weekly*, November 3, 1917, The NYBG newspaper files.

30. "Gardeners of Service Men" *The Evening* Sun, April 15, 1919, The NYBG newspaper file.

31. *The New York Herald*, March 27, 1923, The NYBG newspaper file.

32. *The New York Times*, January 6, 1925; *New York Herald Tribune*, January 9, 1925; *New York Evening Journal*, March 19, 1925; *The New York Times*, March 29, 1925, The NYBG newspaper file.

33. *The Home News*, December 13, 1925, The NYBG newspaper file.

34. "Around the World with Flowers", *New York Sun*, August 25, 1926, The NYBG newspaper file.

35. *The Home News*, August 29, 1926, The NYBG newspaper file.

36. *The New York Times*, October 3, 1926, The NYBG newspaper file.

37. *The Home News*, January 16, 1928, The NYBG newspaper file.

38. *Miami Daily News and Metropolis*, January 19, 1928,The NYBG newspaper file.

39. *Ibid*.

40. *New York Evening Post*, March 23, 1928, The NYBG newspaper file.

41. *New York Times*, June 7, 1929; *Evening World*, June 8, 1929, The NYBG newspaper file.

Certainly N. L. Britton is worthy of a biographical study. His successor, as Secretary/Director, Elmer Drew Merrill, has left us some interesting remarks, which might someday entice someone to provide such a study. After merely touching upon his work as an explorer, researcher, teacher and publisher, he wrote:

> After all is said and done, in spite of Doctor Britton's notable contributions to botanical science, his greatest achievement was undoubtedly the establishment and development of the New York Botanical Garden, a living monument to his memory. The institution was his in a very real sense, and to it he devoted his best efforts through much of his productive life.

See: E.D. Merrill "Biographical Memoir of Britton", *op. cit*. This brief biographical sketch of thirteen pages is followed by forty two pages of his publications. See: *New York Herald Tribune*, June 26, 1934, for the announcement of Dr. Britton's death on June 25, 1934. The 1934 article also describes in considerable detail his life and work.

Chapter VI: The Depression Years

1. *The Home News*, July 21, 1929, Brooklyn, N.Y. *Citizen*, July 17, 1929, The NYBG newspaper file.

2. *Ibid.,* July 28, 1929, The NYBG newspaper file.

3. *Ibid*., October 13, 1929,The NYBG newspaper file.

4. *Ibid*., October 5, 1930, The NYBG newspaper file.

5. Elmer Merrill, "Report of the Secretary and Director—in—Chief for the Year 1930", *Bulletin of The New York Botanical Garden* (Vol. 14, #53, 1931), 257—259.

6. Elmer Merrill, "Report of Secretary and Director—in—Chief for the Year 1931", *Bulletin of The New York Botanical Garden* (Vol. 14, #54, May, 1931); *New York Evening Journal*, June 22, 1932; *New York World Telegram*, September 23, 1932, The NYBG newspaper file.

7. E. R. Merrill, "Annual Report of the Director for the Year 1933", *Journal of The New York Botanical Garden* (Vol. XXXV, #412, April 1934), 65—81.

8. In July, 1935, The Garden reported that Merrill resigned to accept the appointment of Professor of Botany and chief administrator of the botanical collections at Harvard University. See: *Journal of The New York Botanical Garden* (Vol. XXXVI, #427, July, 1935), 162. On July 29, 1935, Dr. Marshall Avery Howe, who had been the Assistant Director for the past twelve years and Editor of the *Journal* since 1924, was elected Director. See: *Journal of the New York Botanical Garden* (Vol. XXXVI, #428, August, 1935), 188. On December 24, 1936, Marshall A. Howe died at his home in Pleasantville, New York, at the age of seventy. He had been Director of The Garden for less than fifteen months. See: *Journal of The New York Botanical Garden* (Vol. XXXVIII, #446, February, 1937). He was succeeded by Dr. William J. Robbins.

9. M. A. Howe, "Annual Report of the Director for the Year 1935", *Journal of The New York Botanical Garden* (Vol. XXXVII, #436, April, 1936), 77.

10. "WPA Helped to Arrange Biblical Flower Exhibit", *The Home News*, March, 1941, The NYBG newspaper file.

11. *The New York Botanical Garden Journal* (Vol. XXXIII, #395. November, 1932), 251—255.

12. *Florists Exchange and Horticultural Trade World*, April 14, 1934, The NYBG newspaper file.

13. "New Gardening Courses Begin In March", *Journal of The New York Botanical Garden* (Vol. XXXIX, #458, February, 1938), 39—41.

14. *Journal of The New York Botanical Garden* (Vol. 41, #481, January, 1940), 18—19.

15. See: "Herbarium Receives 2,000,000th Specimen At Ceremony Following Addresses"; John Hendley Barnhart, "History of the Garden Herbarium", *Journal of The New York Botanical Garden* (Vol. 42, #493, January, 1941), 19—21; "The Herbarium of The New York Botanical Garden", *Science*, December 2, 1940, The NYBG newspaper file.

Chapter VII: World War II

1. Robbins was absolutely correct. By the end of 1942 The Garden had lost about 25% of its male employees. Some joined the armed forces and others were attracted by war work in various factories. Still others answered the call of government agencies and private industries seeking trained botanists and horticulturists to work on developing substitutes for various materials in short supply as a result of the war. See: William J. Robbins, "Annual Report of the Director for 1942", *Journal of The New York Botanical Garden* (Vol. 44, #522, June, 1943), 2—3.

2. William J. Robbins, "The Garden and The War", *Journal of The New York Botanical Garden* (Vol. 43, #505, January, 1942).

3. James S. Jack, "Practical Vegetable Growing For Amateur Gardeners", *Journal of The New York Botanical Garden* (Vol. 43, #505, January 1942), 1—5.

4. "Instruction Begun in War Gardening", *The New York Times*, January 29, 1942,The NYBG newspaper file.

5. *Journal of The New York Botanical Garden* (Vol. 43, #513, September, 1942).

6. "The Garden's War Work", *Journal of The New York Botanical Garden* (Vol. 44, #520, April, 1943), 93—94; William J. Robbins, "Annual Report of the Director for 1943", *Journal of The New York Botanical Garden* (Vol. 45, #532, April, 1944). For a more detailed description of the program for the anti—aircraft units, see: "The Garden—Club Boys", *The New Yorker*, April 17, 1943, The NYBG newspaper file.

7. "Botanists at War", *The New Yorker*, September 18, 1943, The NYBG newspaper file.

8. Geoffrey T. Hellman, "Square Deal Among the Fungi, A Profile", *op. cit.*, July 19, 1947, The NYBG Scrapbook, Box #15, dated 1950—1955.

9. "In Our Nation's Service", *The Garden Journal of The New York Botanical Garden* (Vol. I, #2, March/April, 1951), 55. The article did not mention the solutions discovered for these problems.

10. "Red Cross Display Attracts 100,000 Visitors to Garden", *Journal of The New York Botanical Garden* (Vol. 46, April, 1945), 92—95.

Chapter VIII: Fiftieth Anniversary Celebration

1. "Fiftieth Anniversary FACTS About the New York Botanical Garden", A brochure with no author, Scrapbook #15 in The NYBG newspaper file. This brochure, henceforth referred to as "FACTS", is an excellent self—study of The Garden and certainly deserving a review of its contents.

2. "FACTS", 10.

3. *Ibid.*, 3.

4. *Ibid.*, 3—4.

5. *Ibid.*, 4—8.

6. *Ibid.*, 9.

7. *Ibid.*, 9—10.

8. *Ibid.*, 10—11.

9. *Ibid.*, 11—14.

10. *The New York Times*, May 14, 1945, The NYBG newspaper file.

11. *Ibid.*

12. *Ibid.*, May 20, 1945, The NYBG newspaper file.

13. "Garden's Post—War Plans are Announced", *Journal of the New York Botanical Garden* (Vol. 46, #546, June, 1945), 129.

Chapter IX: Post War Years

1. *New York Herald Tribune*, April 14, 1947; *New York Times*, April 14, 1947, The NYBG newspaper file.

2. *The New York Times*, May 11, 1950, The NYBG newspaper file; "In Our Nation's Service", *The Garden Journal of The New York Botanical Garden* (Vol. I, #2, March/April, 1951), 55.

3. William J. Robbins, Director, "The New York Botanical Garden", excerpts from the address given at the Annual Meeting of the Board of Managers and Members of the Corporation on May 10, 1950. *Journal of the New York Botanical Garden* (Vol. 51, #607, July, 1950), 158—162.

4. *Ibid.*

5. Dr. H. A. Gleason, Head Curator, "Reports of the Annual Meeting of the Corporation of The New York Botanical Garden", May 10, 1950, Library of The NYBG, 11—16.

6. *Ibid.*

7. *New York Times*, May 16, 1952; *New York Post*, August 22, 1952, The NYBG newspaper file.

8. Alice Sircom, "The Lorillard Snuff Mill", Press Release, Vertical file of The NYBG.

9. *New York Herald Tribune*, May 20, 25, 1952; *New York Post*, May 20, 1952; *New York Daily News*, May 25, 1952,

10. William J. Robbins, "Report of the Director", from The NYBG newspaper file."Reports of the Annual Meeting", May 20, 1954, The NYBG Library.

11. William J. Robbins, "Report of the Director", from "Reports at the Annual Meeting" of May 17, 1956, 8—11, The NYBG Library.

Chapter X: Growth & Environmental Issues

1. Steere, Dean of the Graduate Division of Stanford University, received his B.S. in 1929, his M.A. in 1931 and his Ph.D. in 1932, all from the University of Michigan. He taught Botany at Temple University in Philadelphia, returned to a teaching position at Michigan and then joined the faculty of the Department of Biological Sciences at Stanford University in California, serving as assistant professor, associate professor, professor and finally as chair of the department.

2. *The Garden Journal of The New York Botanical Garden* (Vol. 8 January/February, 1958), 33.

3. Floritza I. Diaconescu, "The Native Plant Garden at NYBG", *The Garden Journal of The New York Botanical Garden* (Vol. 11, #1, July/August, 1982), 3—4; "The Native Plant Garden of The New York Botanical Garden", *The Garden Journal of The New York Botanical Garden* (July/August, 1961), 145—146.

4. Charles B. Harding, "A Fifteen—Year Review by the President", June 30, 1964, Vertical File of The NYBG, 1—7. In naming the new library wing after Harriet Barnes Pratt, Harding signaled out the honoree in the following terms.

> No words of mine could do justice to the many great contributions Mrs. Pratt has made to the Garden. I call her the uncrowned queen. She has been a constant source of ideas, wise counsel, and drive. She has contributed more than generously to all the major construction projects and at one time by a specific donation made it possible for us to give desperately needed salary increases to our underpaid staff when we had no other funds to draw on. For many years as Chairman of our City Relations Committee, she was responsible for keeping

these relations harmonious and productive. She has been an inspiration to us all and especially to the devoted women who serve as our Advisory Volunteers. It is for these reasons and many others that Mrs. Pratt has twice been given the Distinguished Service Award of the New York Botanical Garden.

5. In 1971 Mrs. Buckner, the daughter of Thomas J. Watson contributed nearly $3 million for the construction of this wing of the Museum Building. Up to 1976 it was the largest donation ever made to The Garden. See: *The New York Times*, February 3, 1976.

6. Elaine C. Cherry, "The New York Botanical Garden: A Registered National Historic Landmark", *Garden Journal* (Vol. 17, #3, May/June, 1967; Vol. 17, #4, July/August 1967), 99—108.

7. *Ibid.*, 99.

8. *Ibid.*, 102.

9. *Ibid.*, 102—104.

10. "Conservation and the Preservation of the Species", *Garden Journal* (Vol. 17, #3, May/June 1967; Vol. 17, #4, July/August 1967), 91—93.

11. *Ibid.*

12. S. H. Hutner, "The Urban Botanical Garden: An Academic Wildlife Preserve", *Garden Journal* (Vol. 19, #2, March/April 1969), 37—40.

13. Ibid.

14. "NYBG Offers Help for Home Gardeners", *Garden Journal* (January/February, 1990), 3—4.

15. *Ibid.*, 3—4.

16. *A Guide to the New York Botanical Garden* (New York: Published by The New York Botanical Garden, 1986), 32.

17. Axel Horn & John Sedgwick, "The Bronx River Project", *Garden Journal* (Vol. 24, #2, April 1974), 61—64. Axel Horn, an artist with many years of employment in graphics and science exhibits, was Coordinator of the Environmental Studies Program Development at The Garden. John Sedgwick was The NYBG's Coordinator of Environmental Education. He had a long association with efforts to purify his native Hudson River. He was Vice President of the Hudson River Fisherman's Association (the most important conservation organization on the waterway), an officer of Hudson River Sloop Restoration, Inc., and an active participant in the Scenic Hudson Preservation Conference that was involved in the Storm King Dispute.

18. Horn and Segwick, "The Bronx River Project", 61.

19. *Ibid.*, 62.

20. *Ibid.*

21. *Ibid.*, 62—63.

22. *Ibid.*, 63.

23. *Ibid.*, 64.

Chapter XI: Conservatory, Library, Herbarium

1. Howard S. Irwin, "The Conservatory: A Third Life", *Garden Journal* (August 1973), 128.

2. *Ibid.*

3. Paul Trachtman, "Bronx 'Crystal Palace'", *Smithsonian* (Washington, Associates, July, 1978), 68.

4. *Ibid.*, 68—69.

5. *Ibid.*

6. *Ibid.*, 70.

7. *Ibid.*, 71.

8. Lesley Oelsner, "$5 Million Gift Restores Conservatory", *The New York Times*, 1978.

9. John F. Reed, Curator of the Library, "The Library of The New York Botanical Garden", *Garden Journal* (May/June 1969), 77—88.

10. *Ibid.*, 79—80.

11. *Ibid.*

12. *Ibid.*, 82—83.

13. *Ibid.*, 86—87.

14. *Ibid.*, 86.

15. "Rare Botanic Scrolls Acquired by Garden", *Riverdale Press*, March 25, 1976.

16. Frank Anderson, "The Springtime of Science, The Twelfth Century Circa Instans", *Garden Journal*, August, 1979.

17. *Ibid.*, 142.

18. Earl Aronson, "Herbarium Plays Role in Research", *Garden Journal*, (August, 1979).

19. *Ibid.*

Index